I0481744

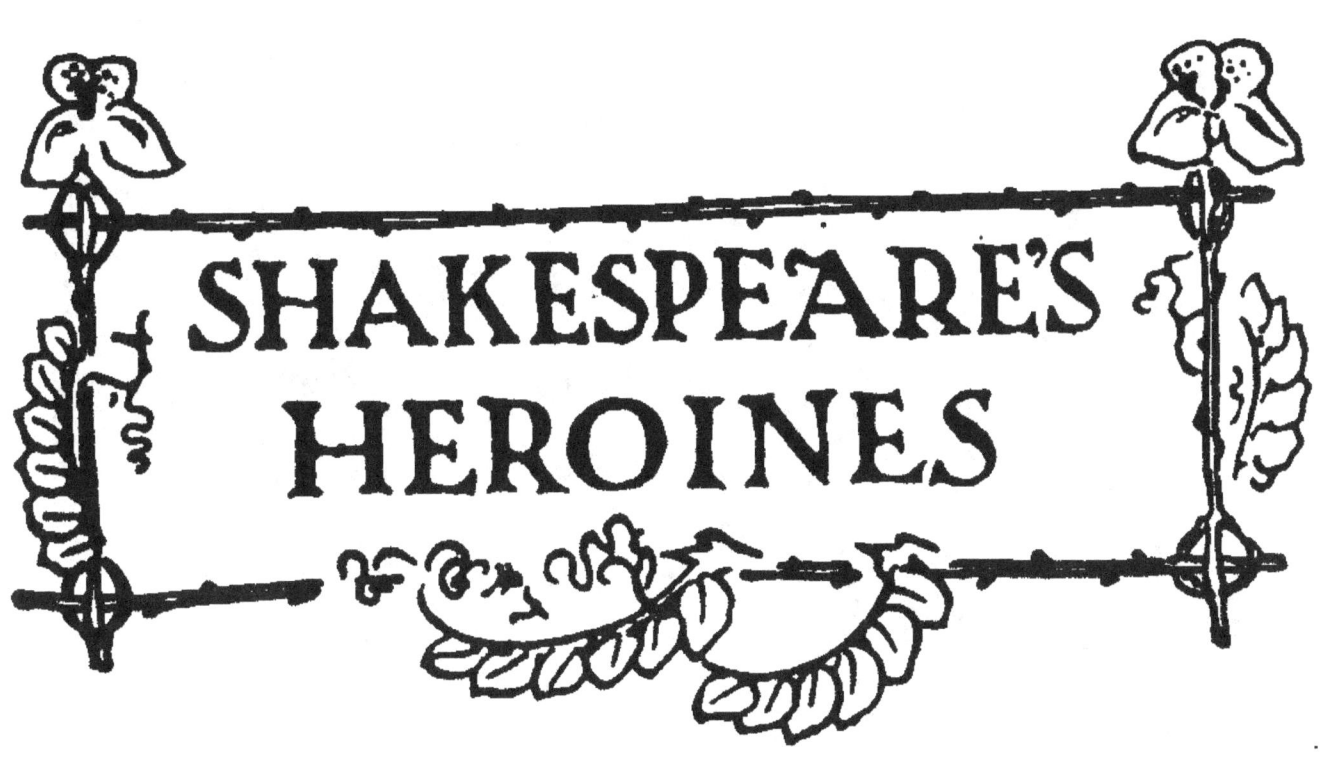

SHAKESPEARE'S HEROINES

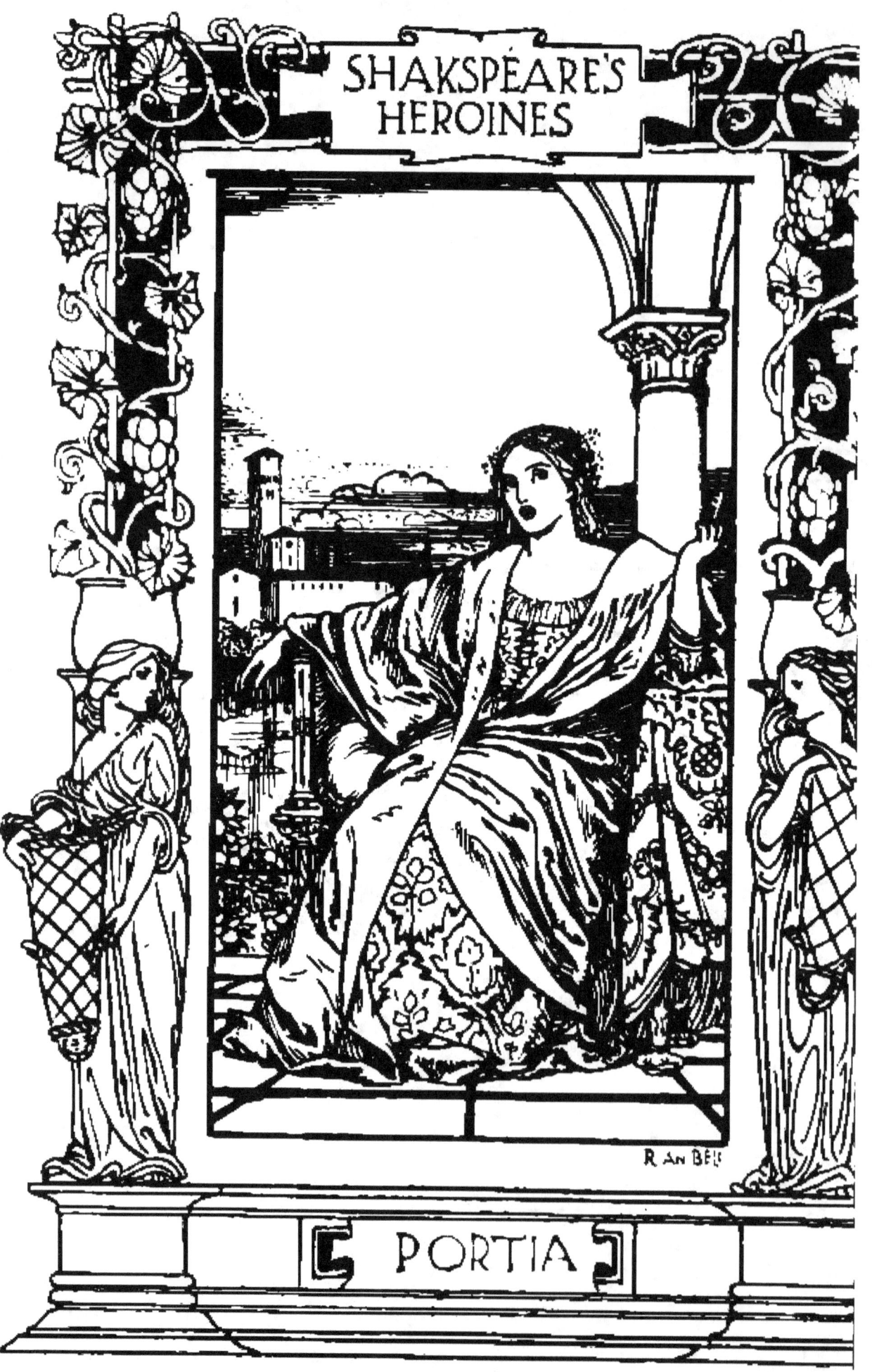

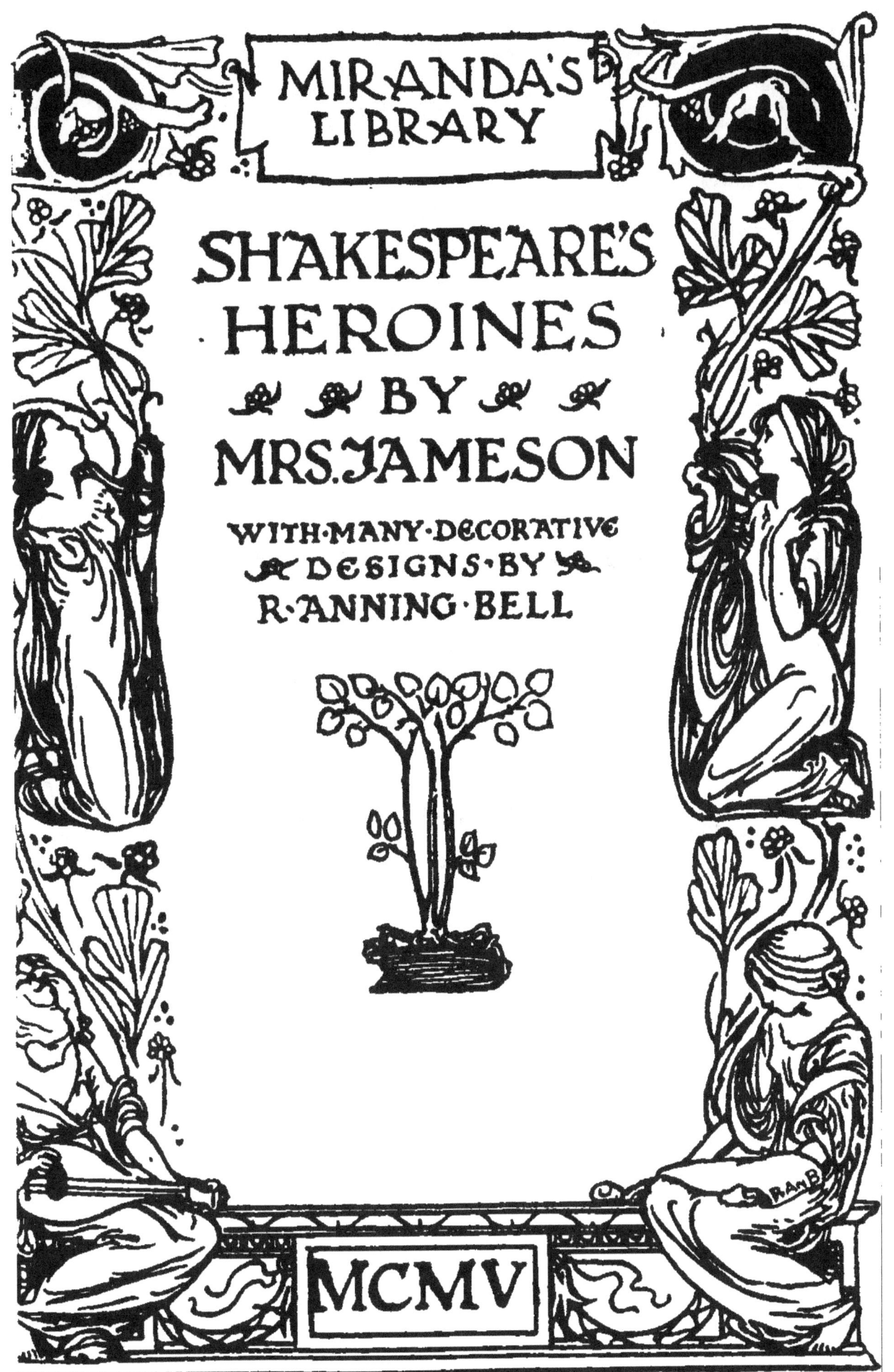

MIRANDA'S
LIBRARY

SHAKESPEARE'S
HEROINES
BY
MRS. JAMESON

WITH·MANY·DECORATIVE
DESIGNS·BY
R·ANNING·BELL

MCMV

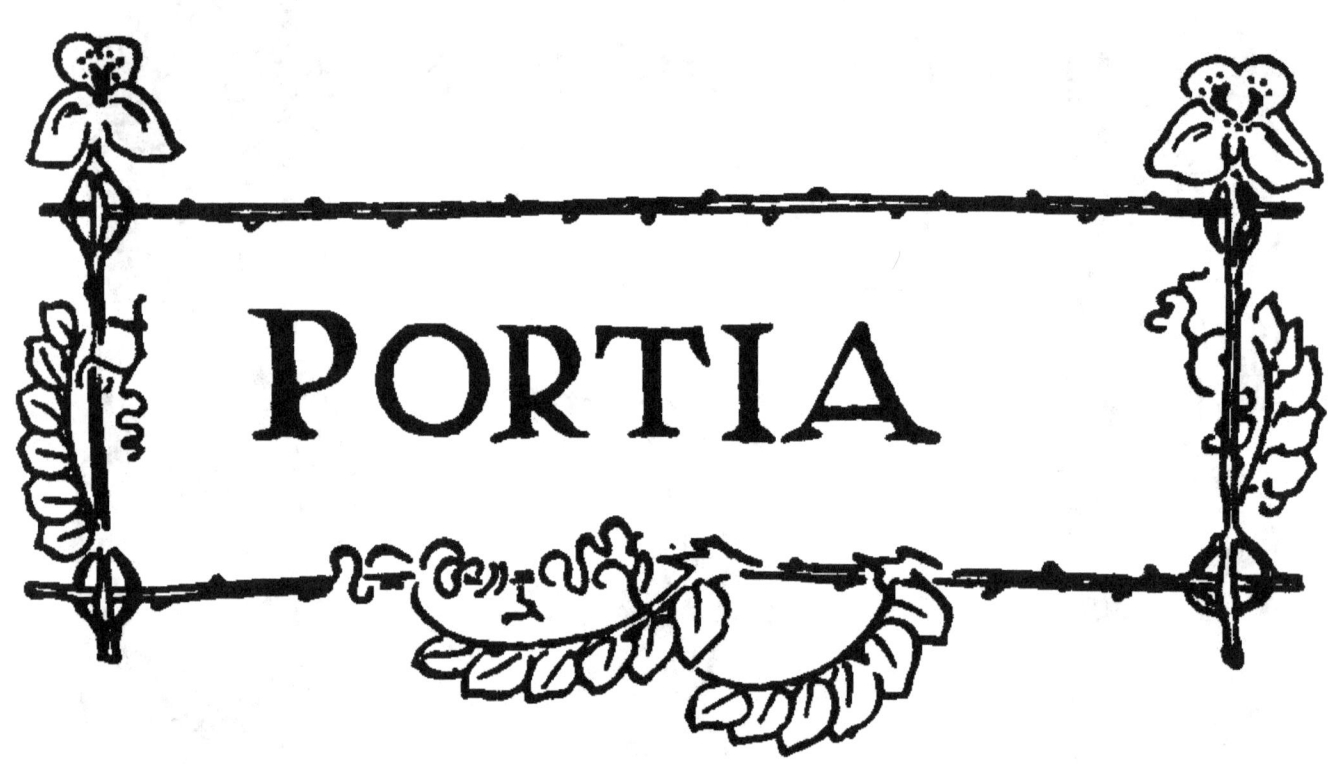

PORTIA

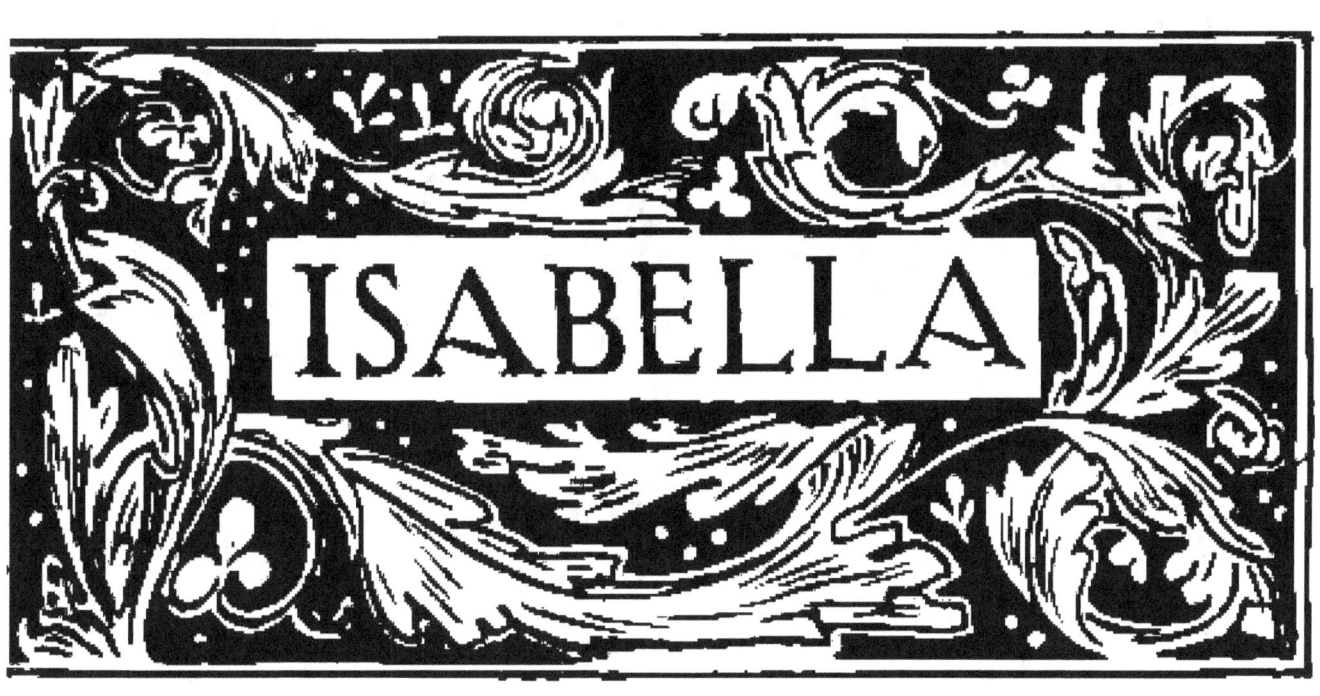

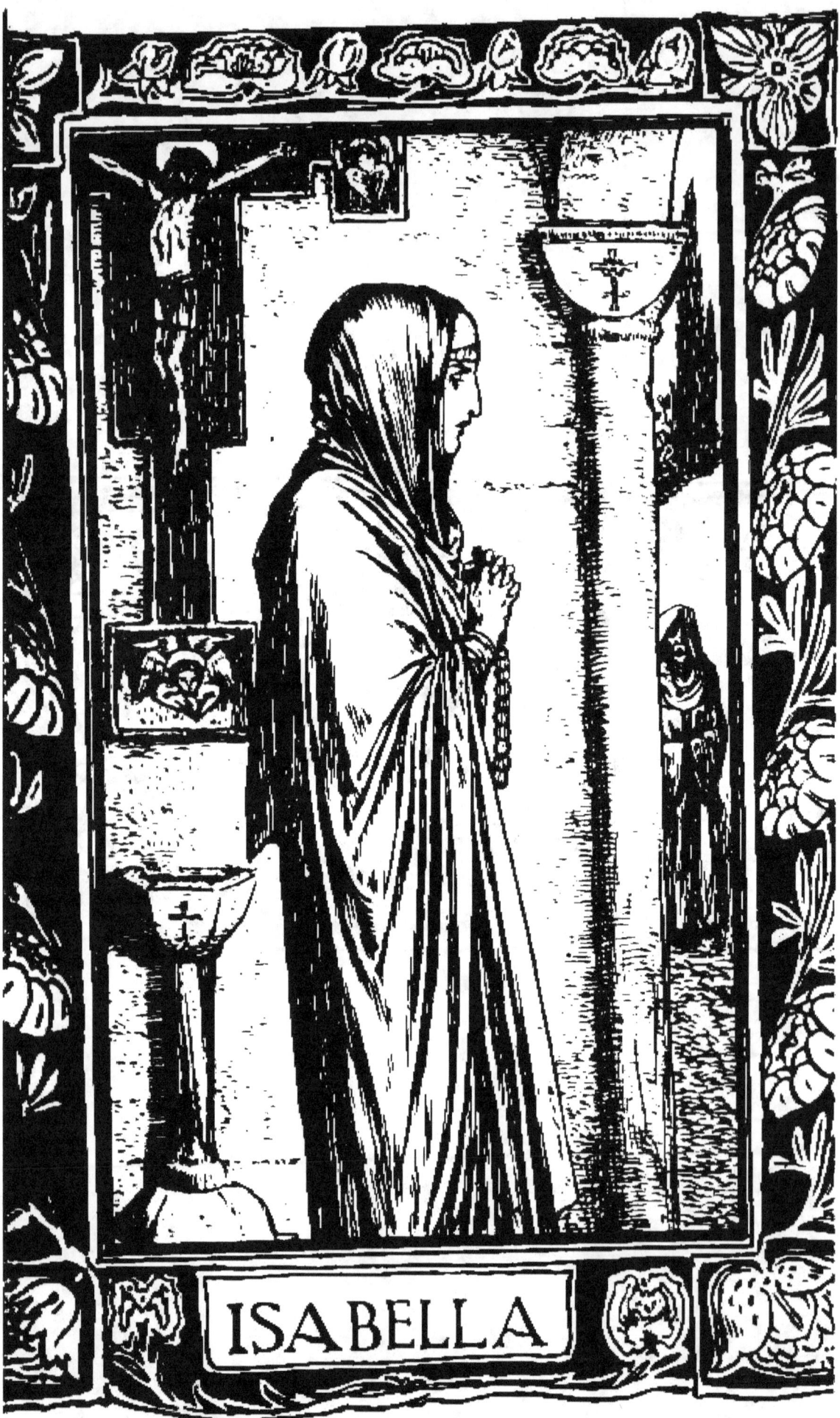

ISABELLA

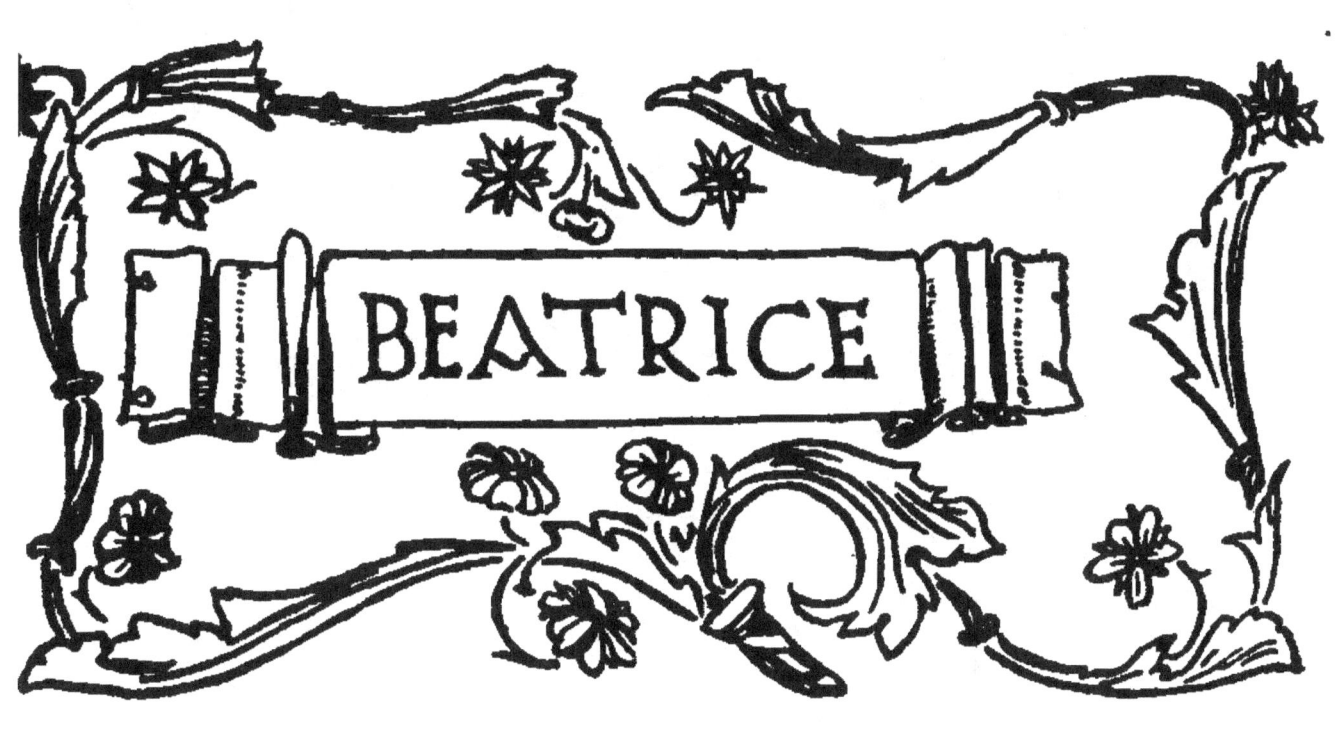

BEATRICE

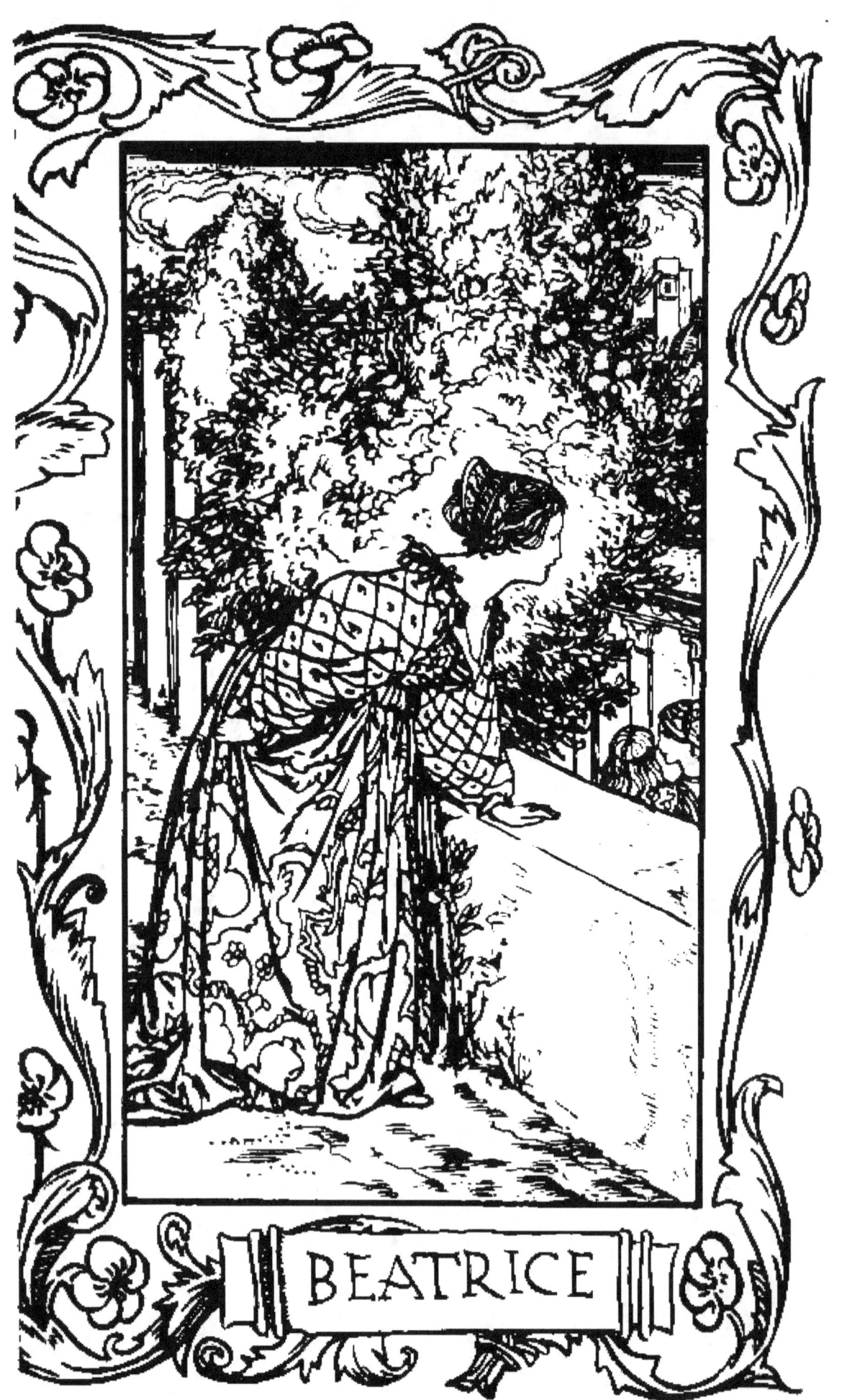

BEATRICE

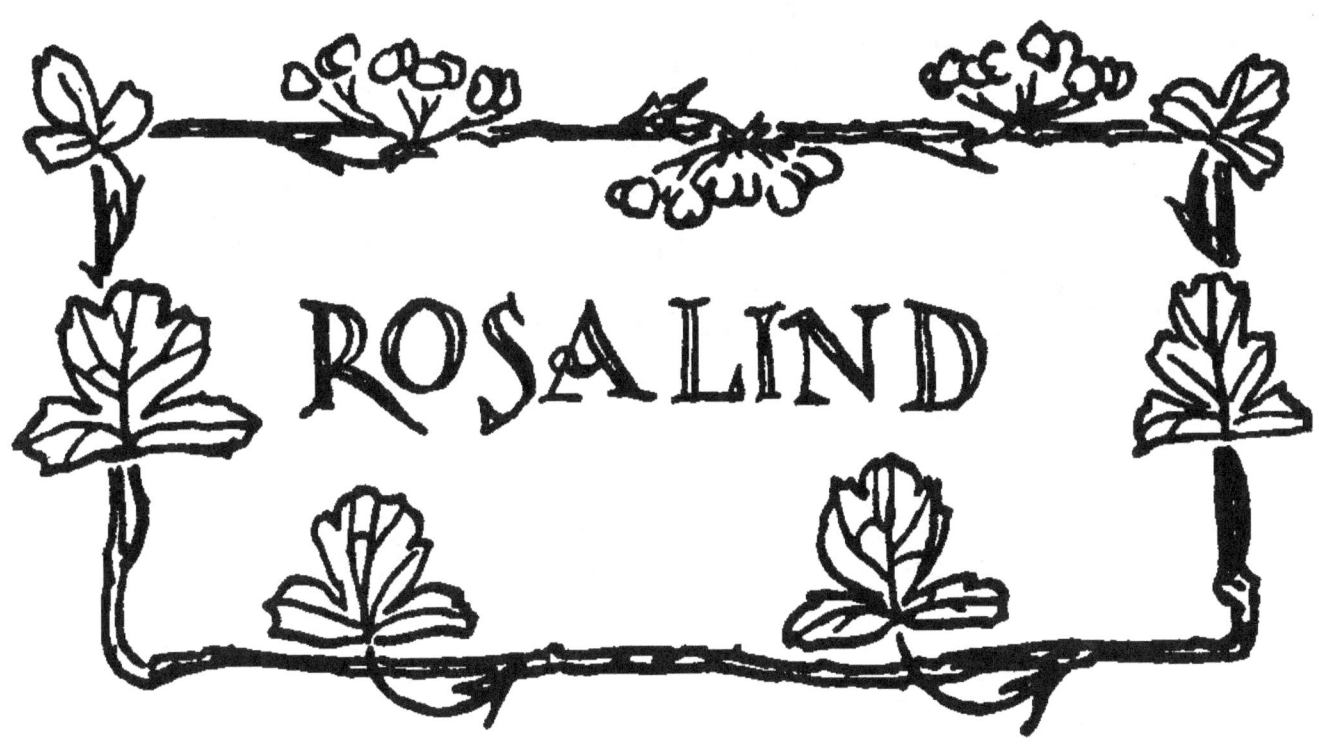

ROSALIND

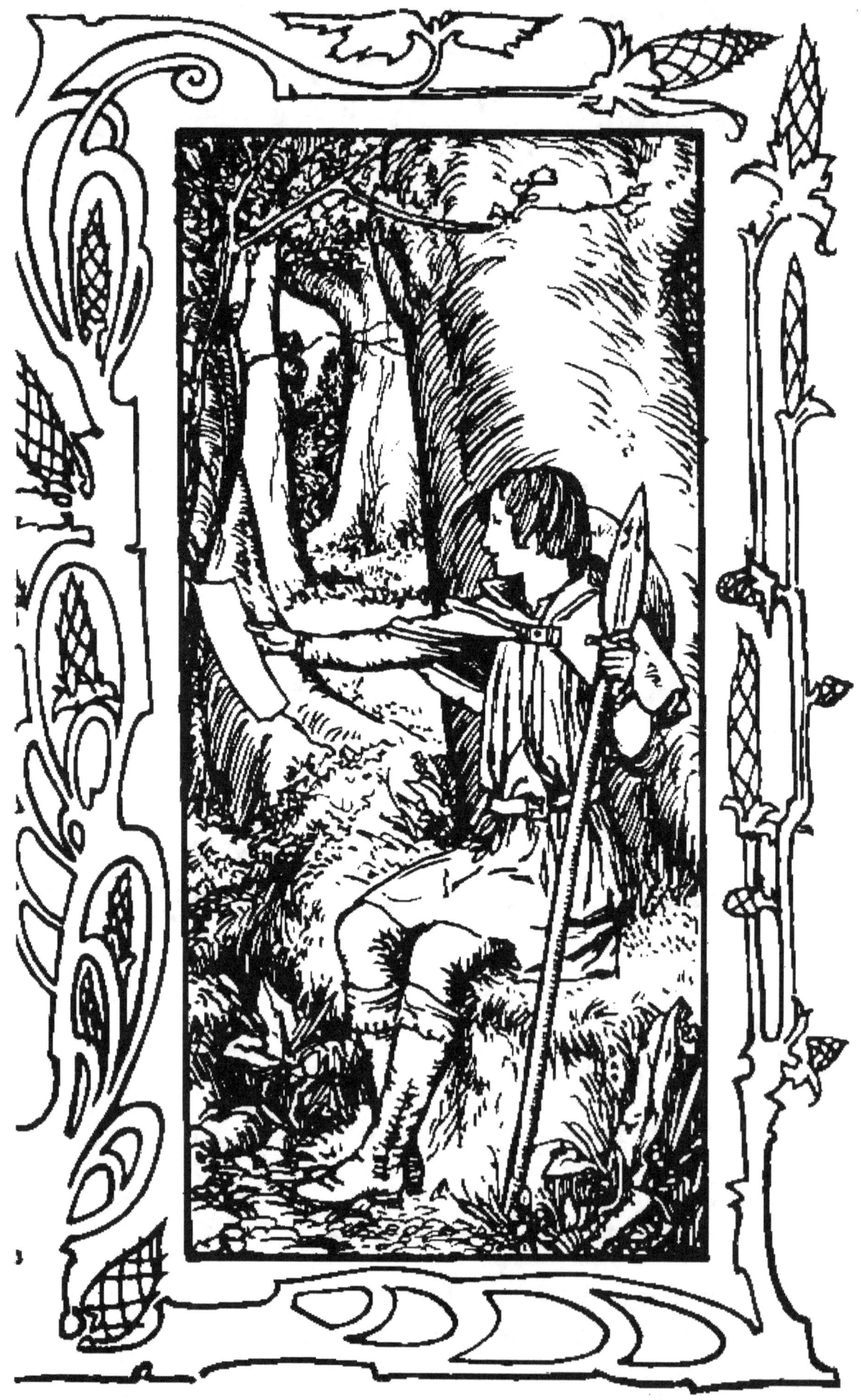

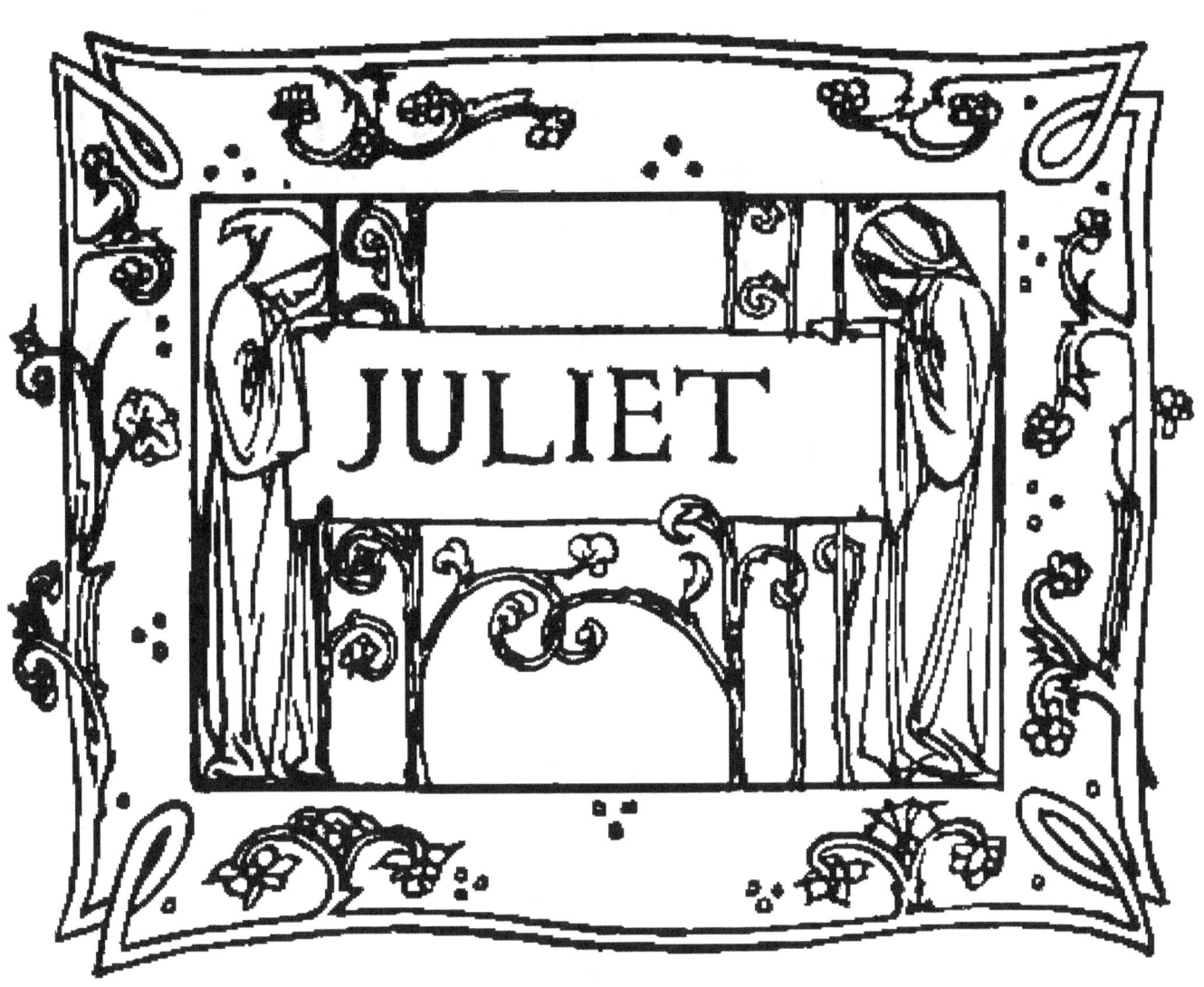

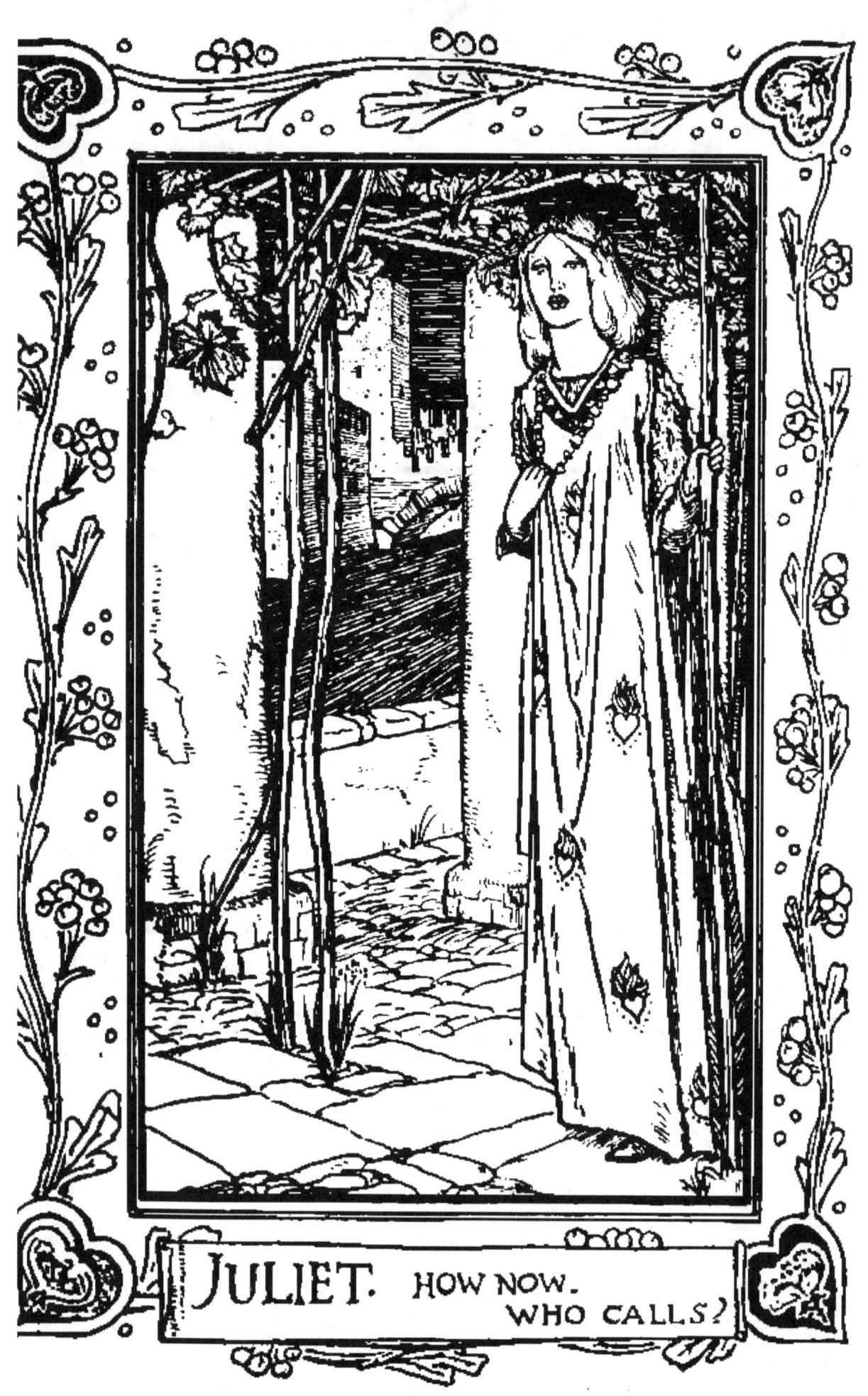

JULIET. HOW NOW.
WHO CALLS?

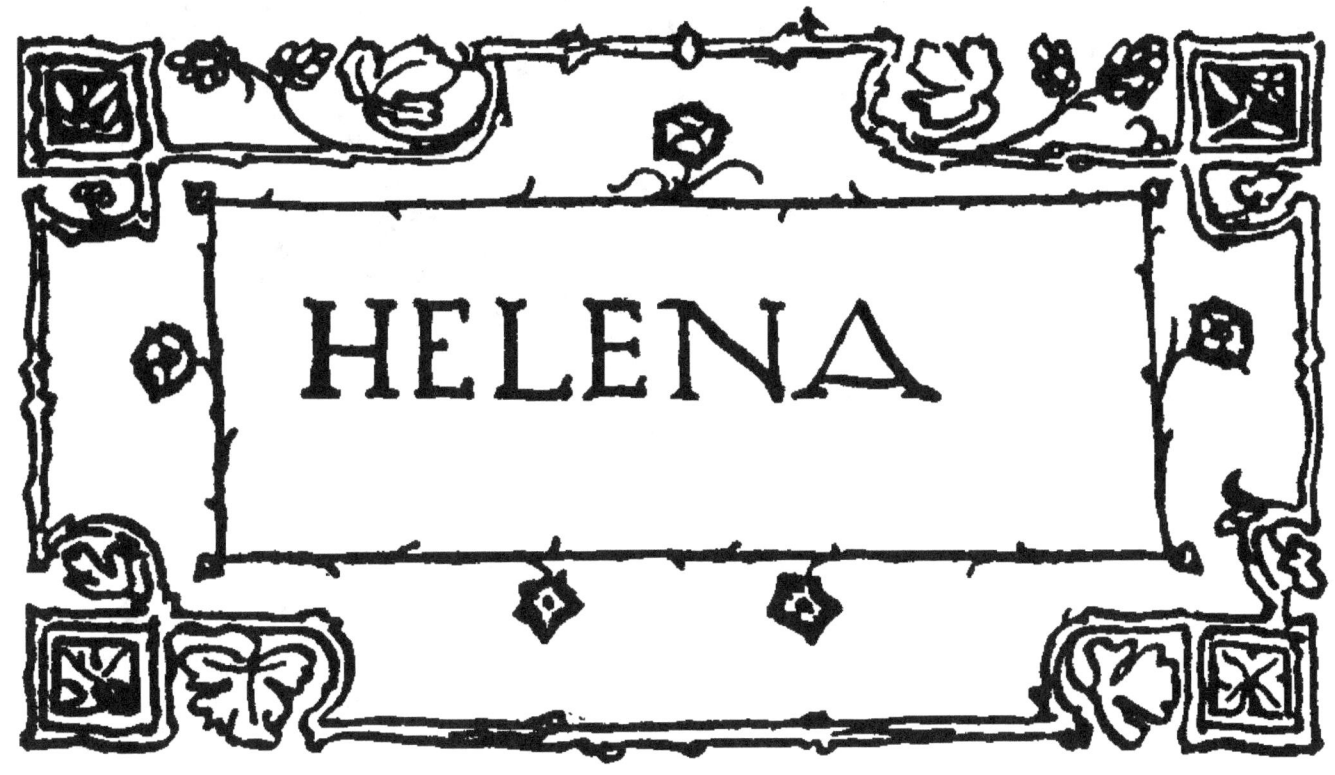

HELENA

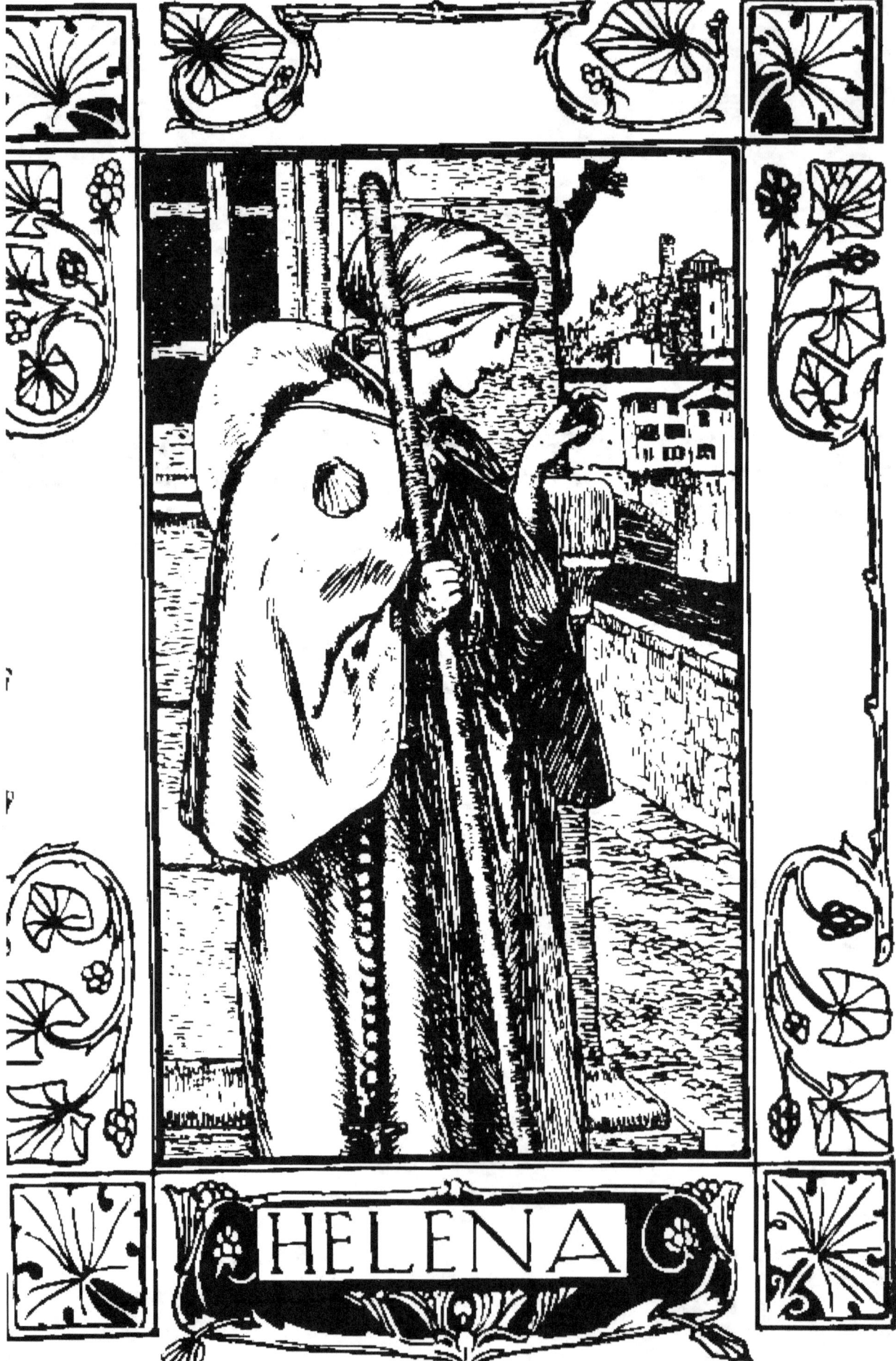

HELENA

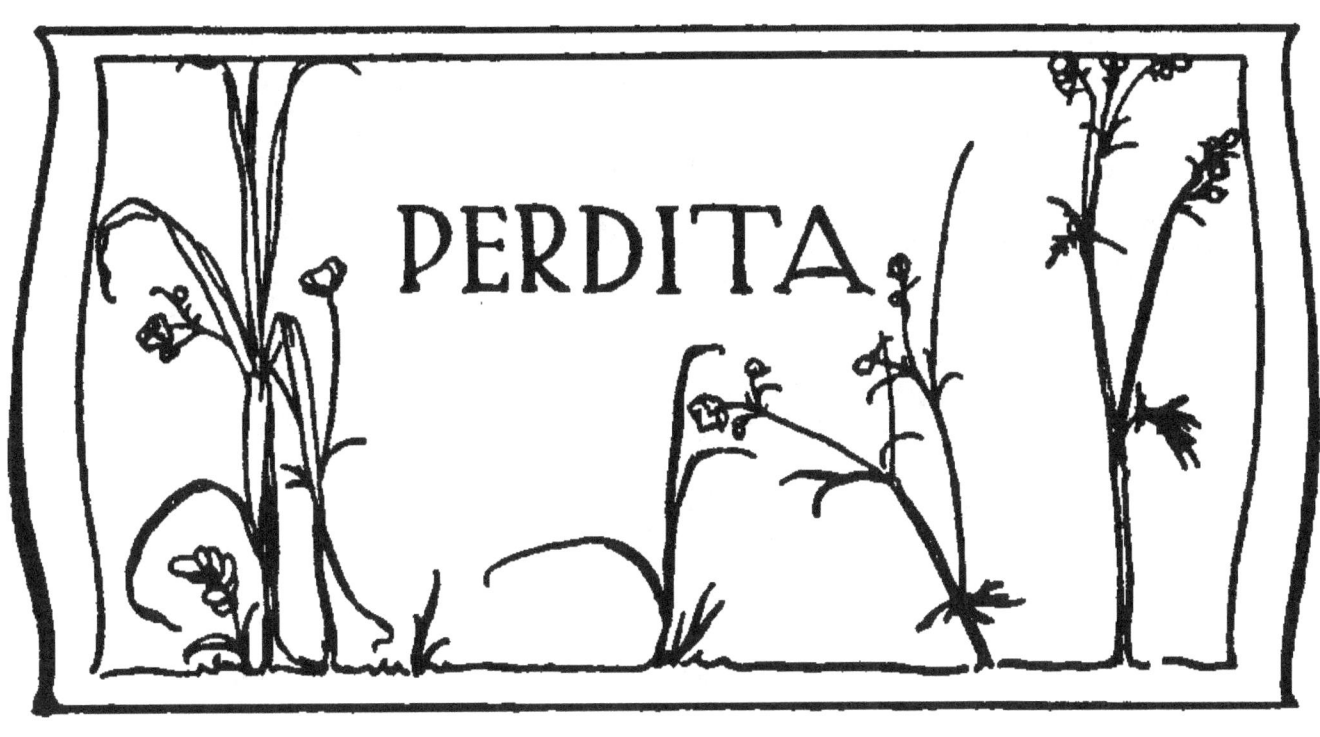

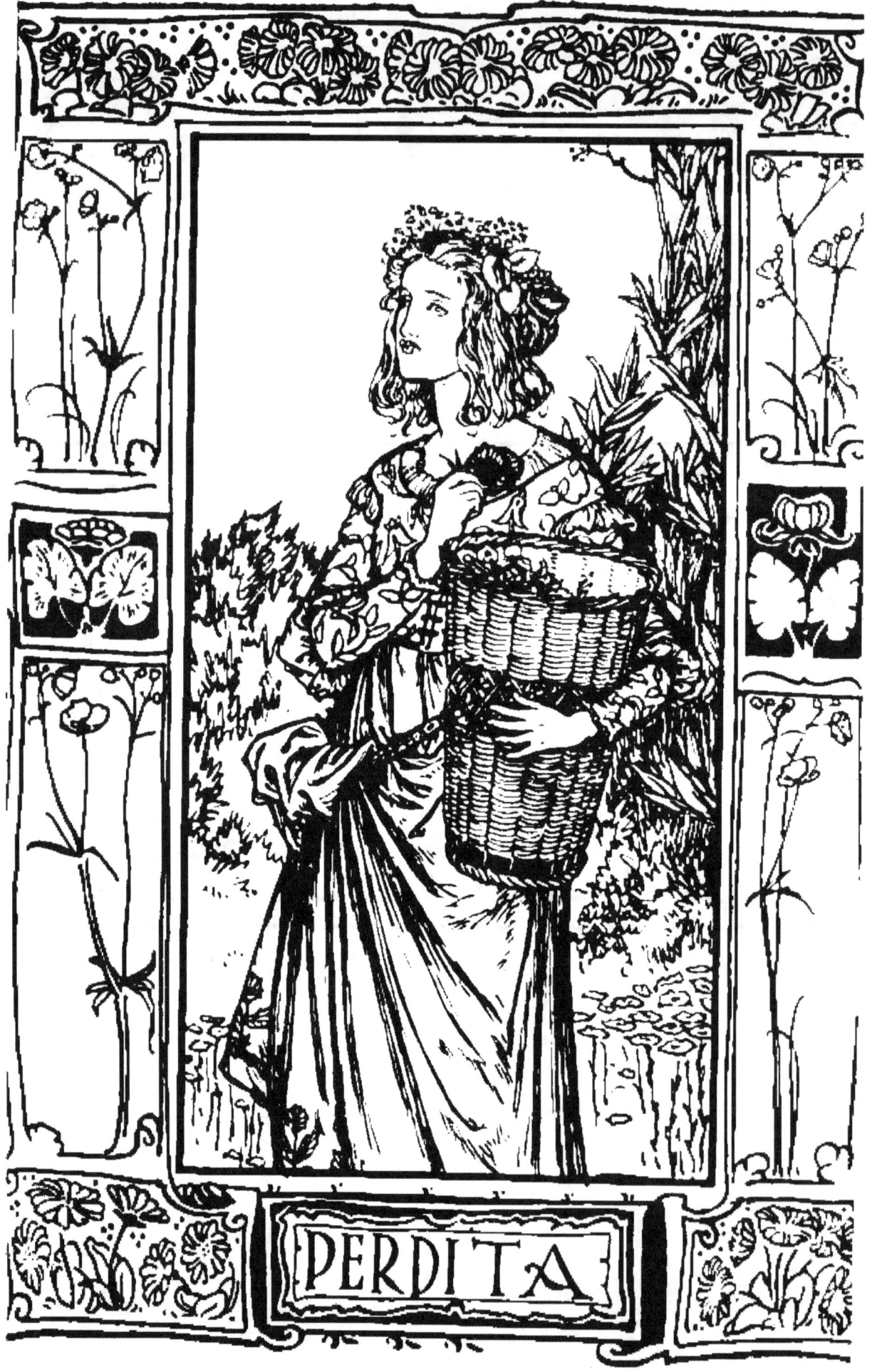

PERDITA

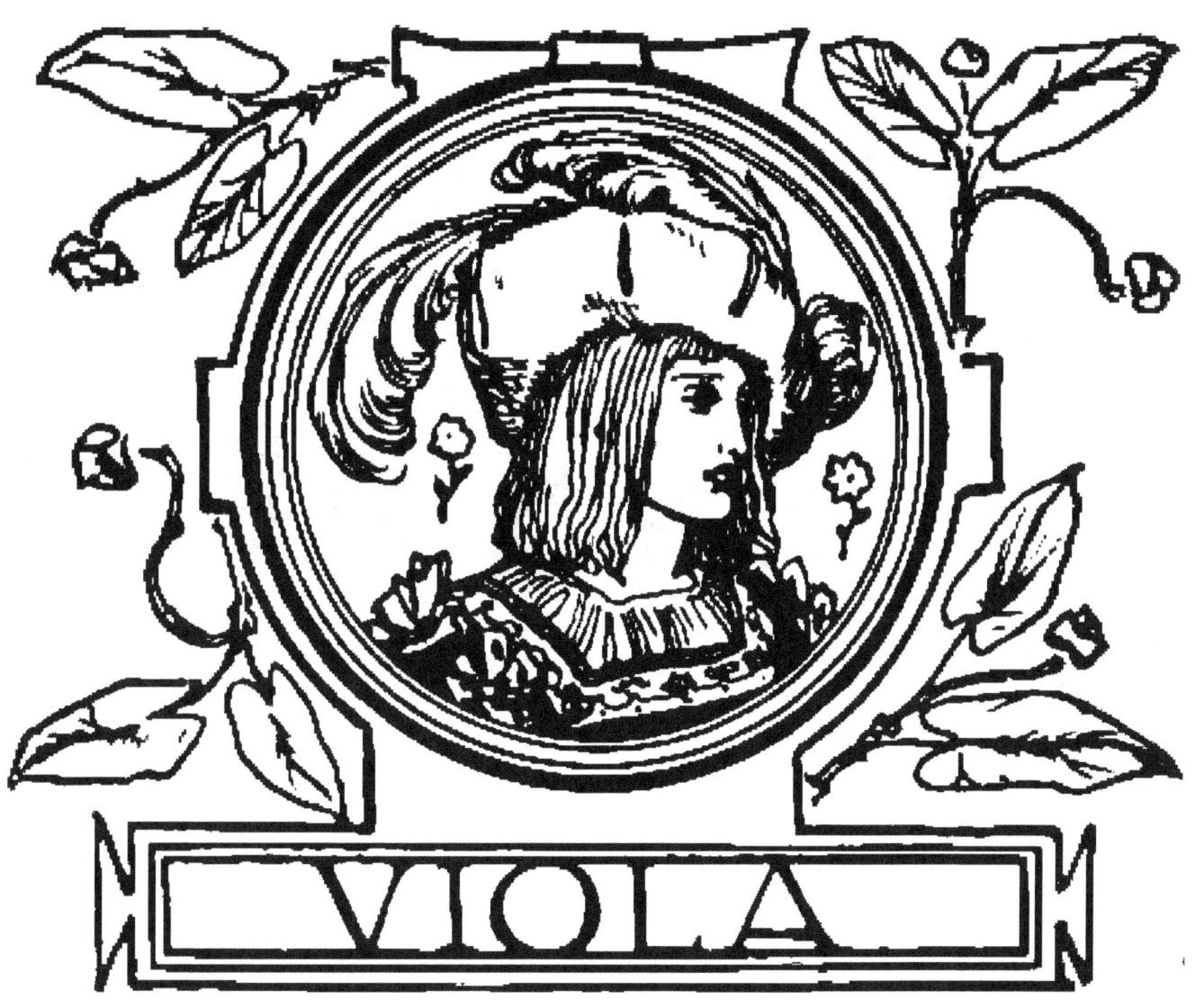

VIOLA

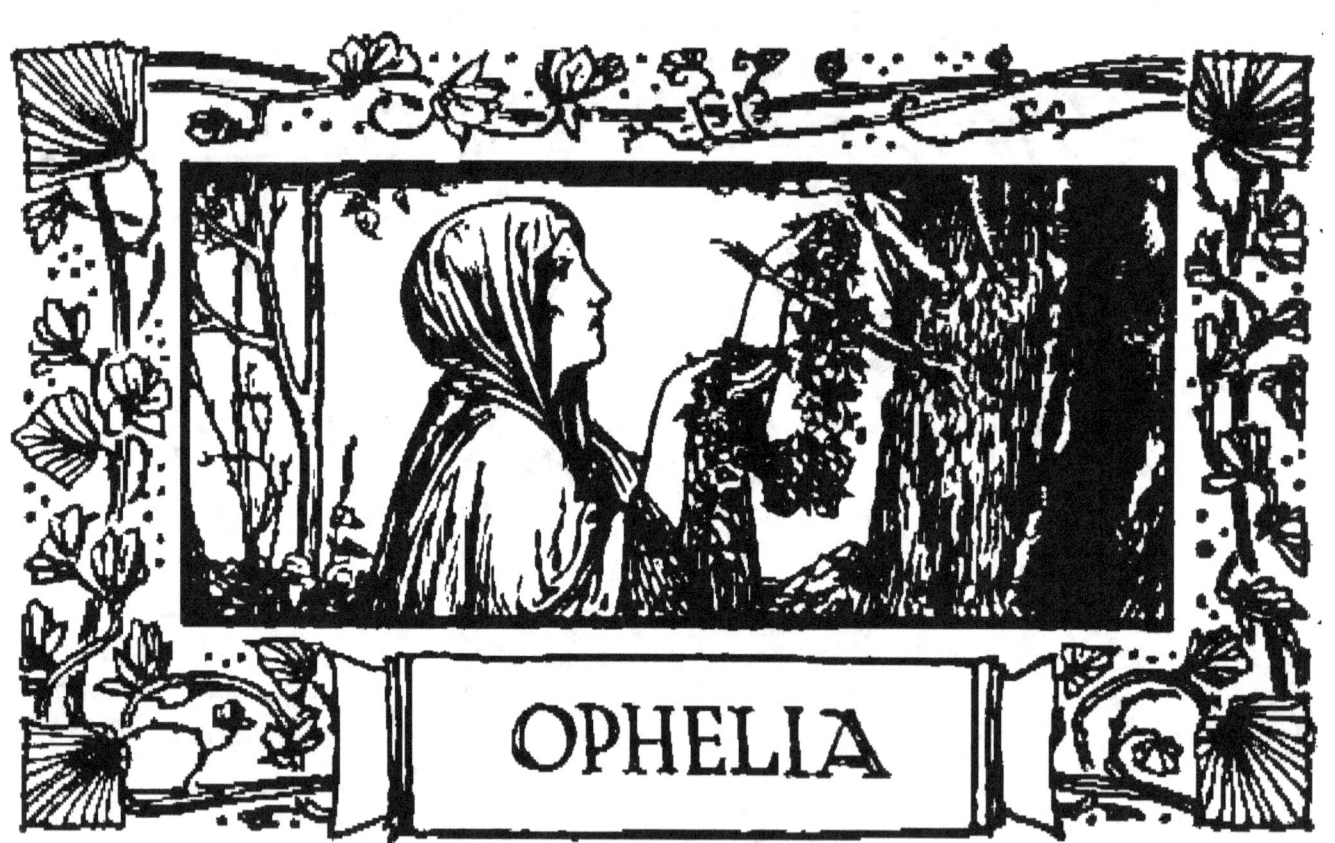

OPHELIA

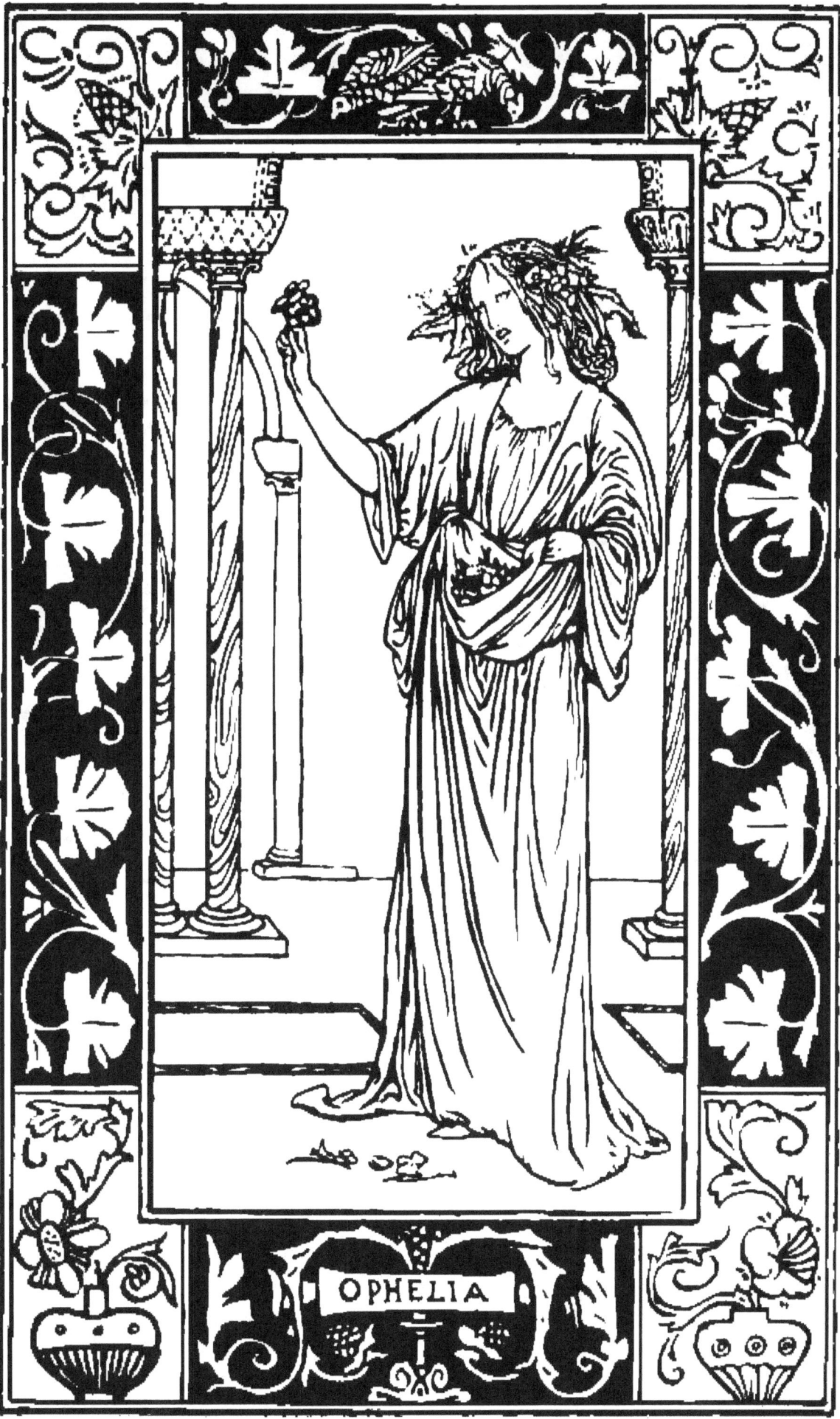

OPHELIA

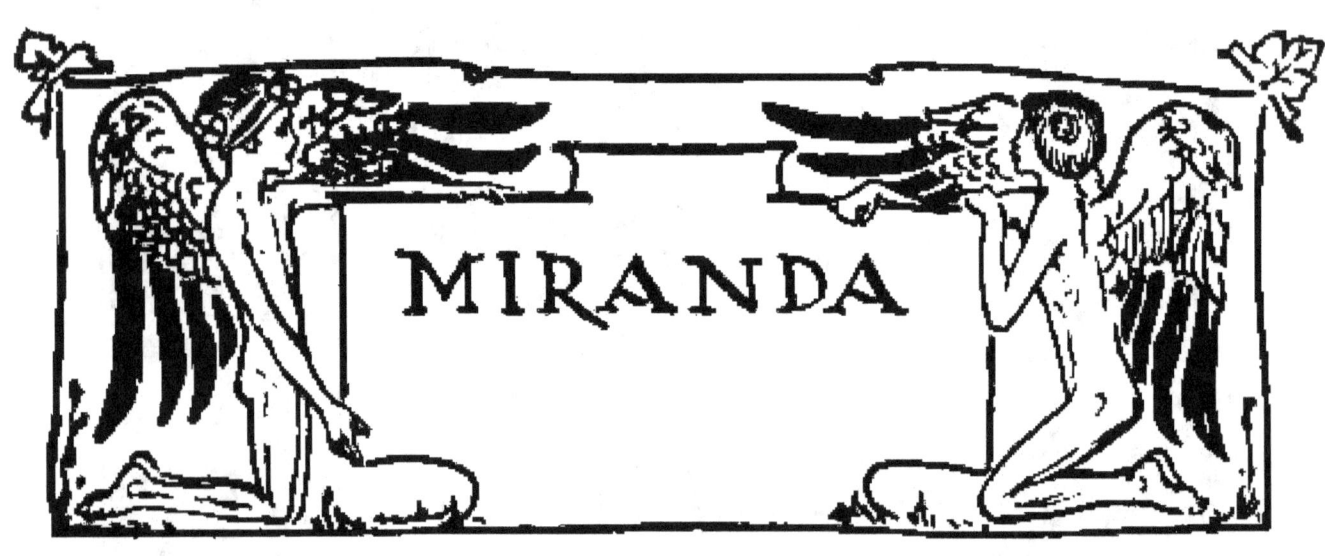

MIRANDA

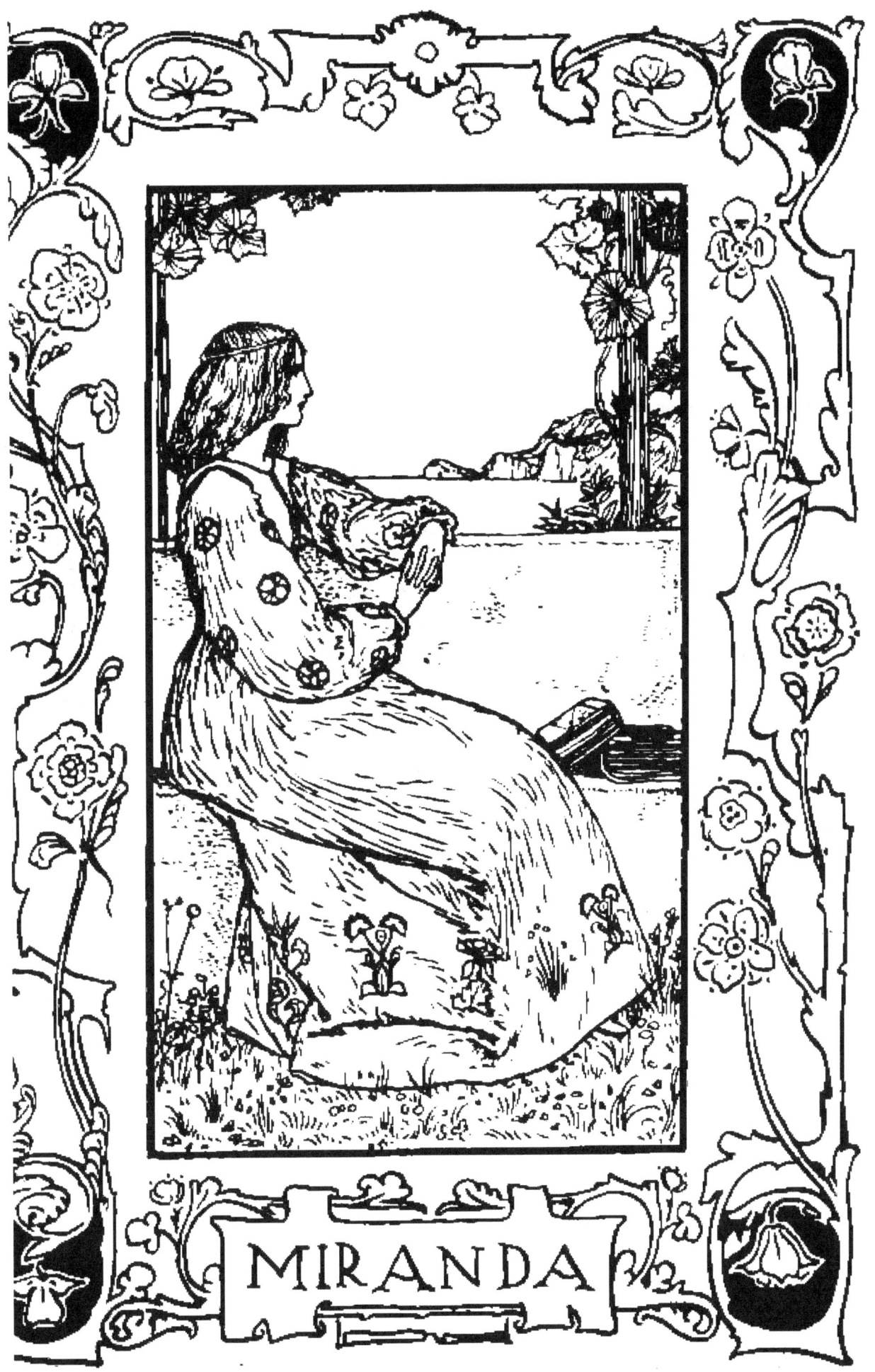

MIRANDA

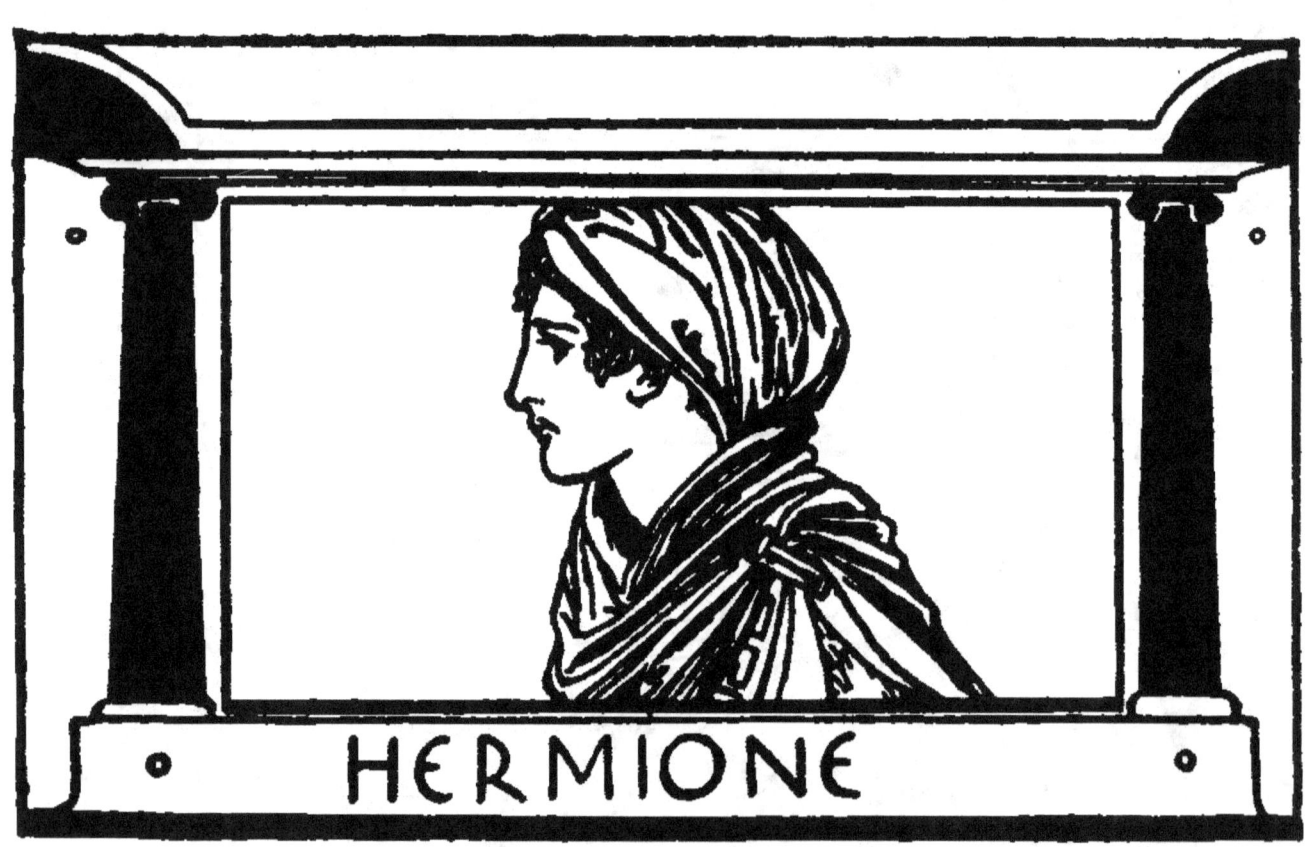

HERMIONE

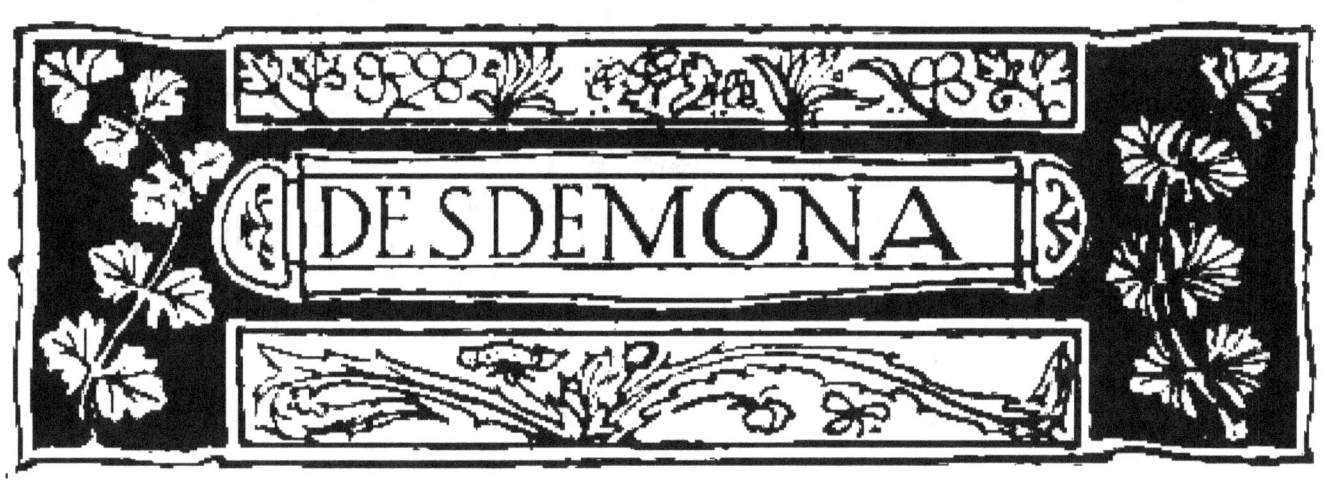

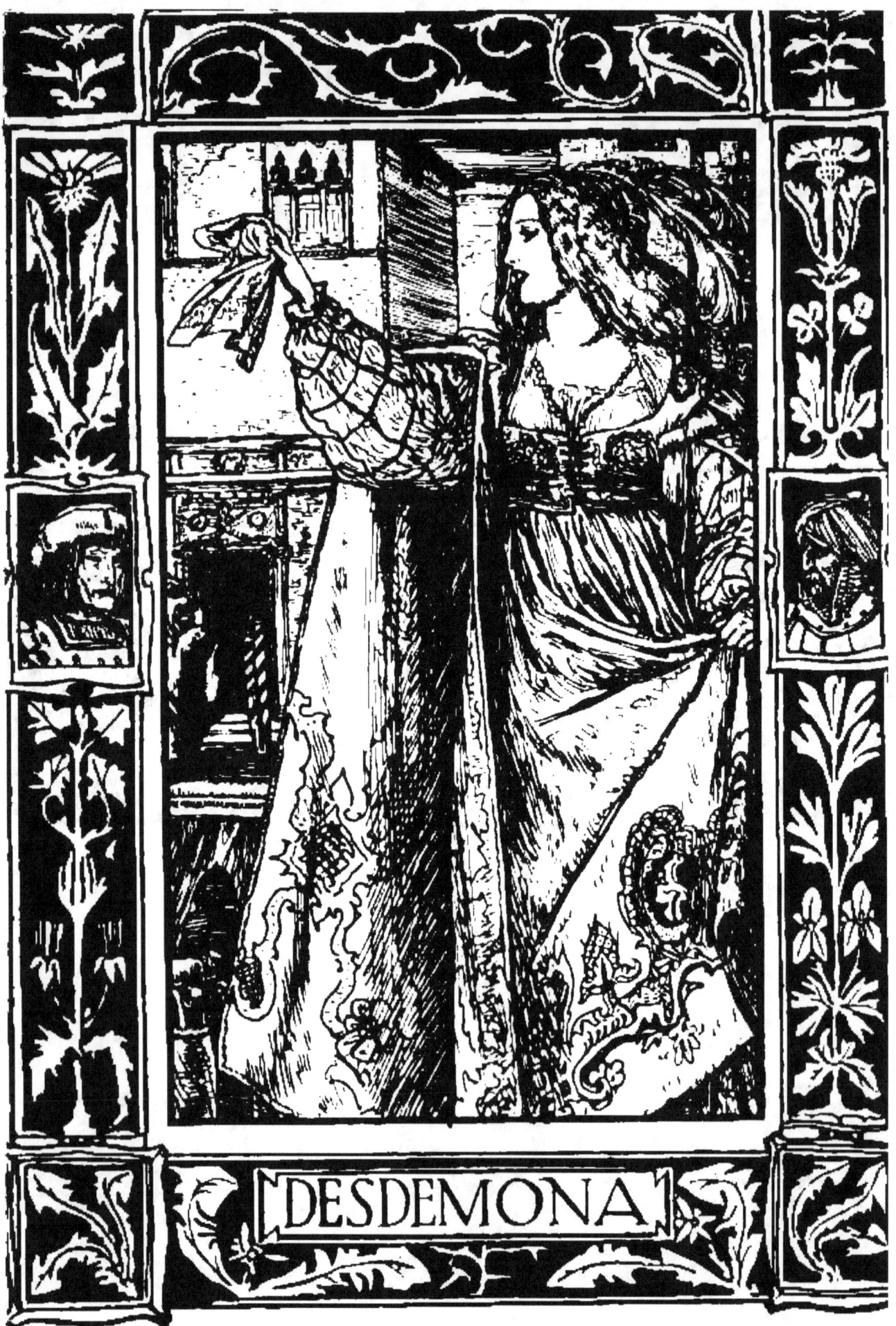

DESDEMONA

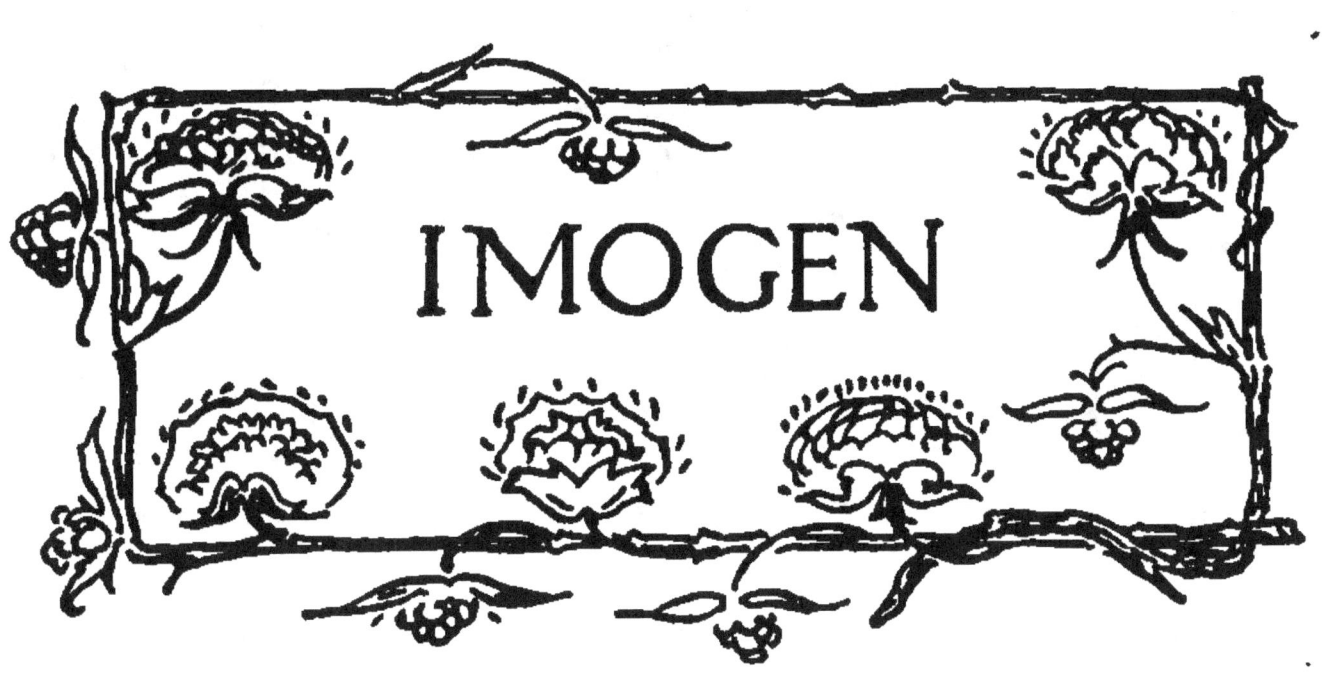

IMOGEN

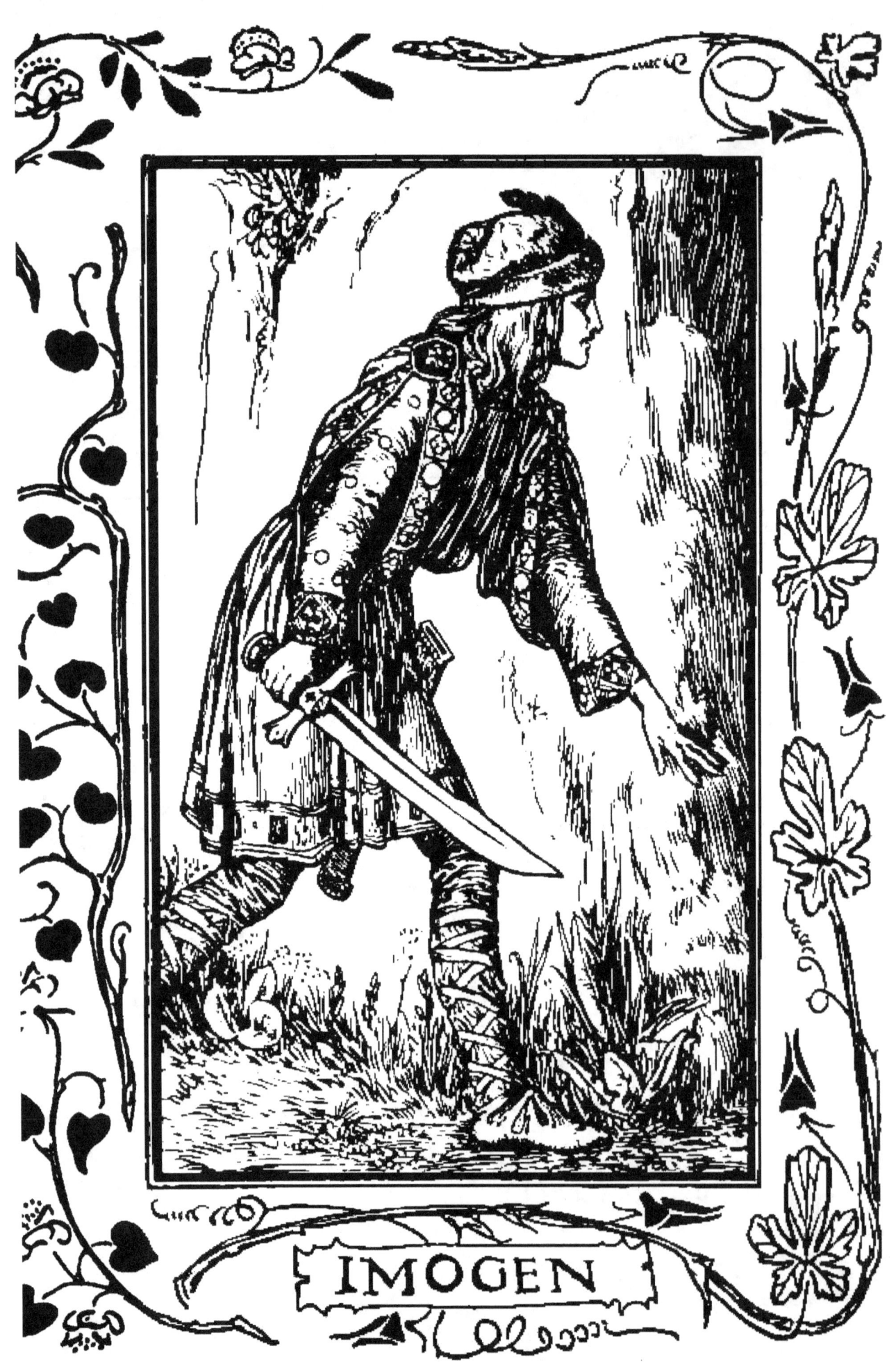

IMOGEN

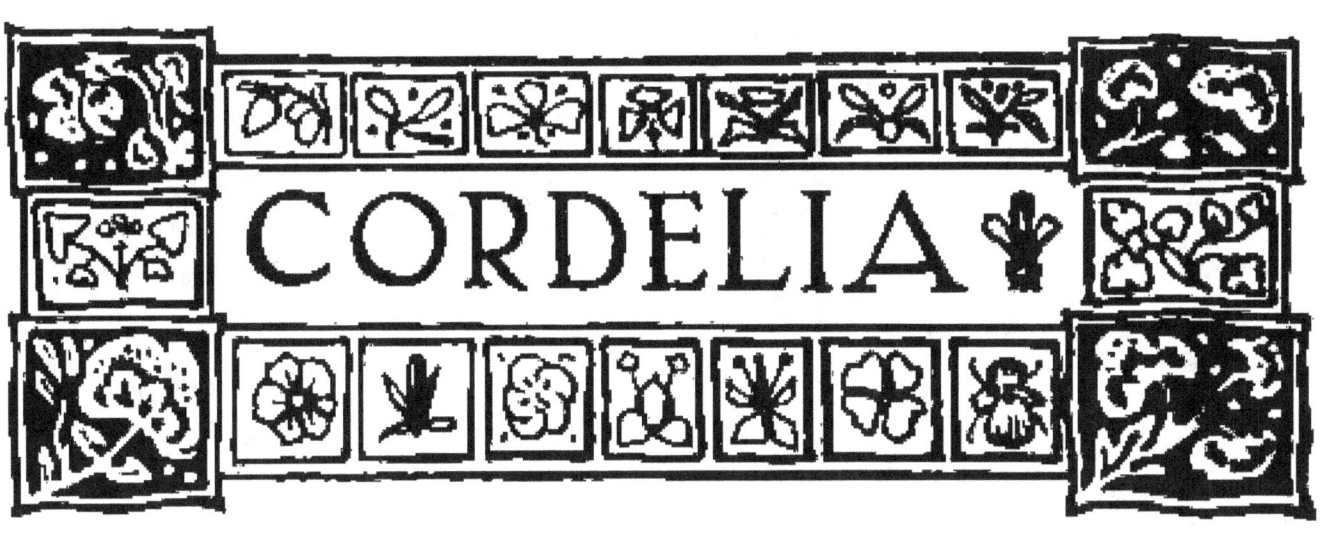

CORDELIA

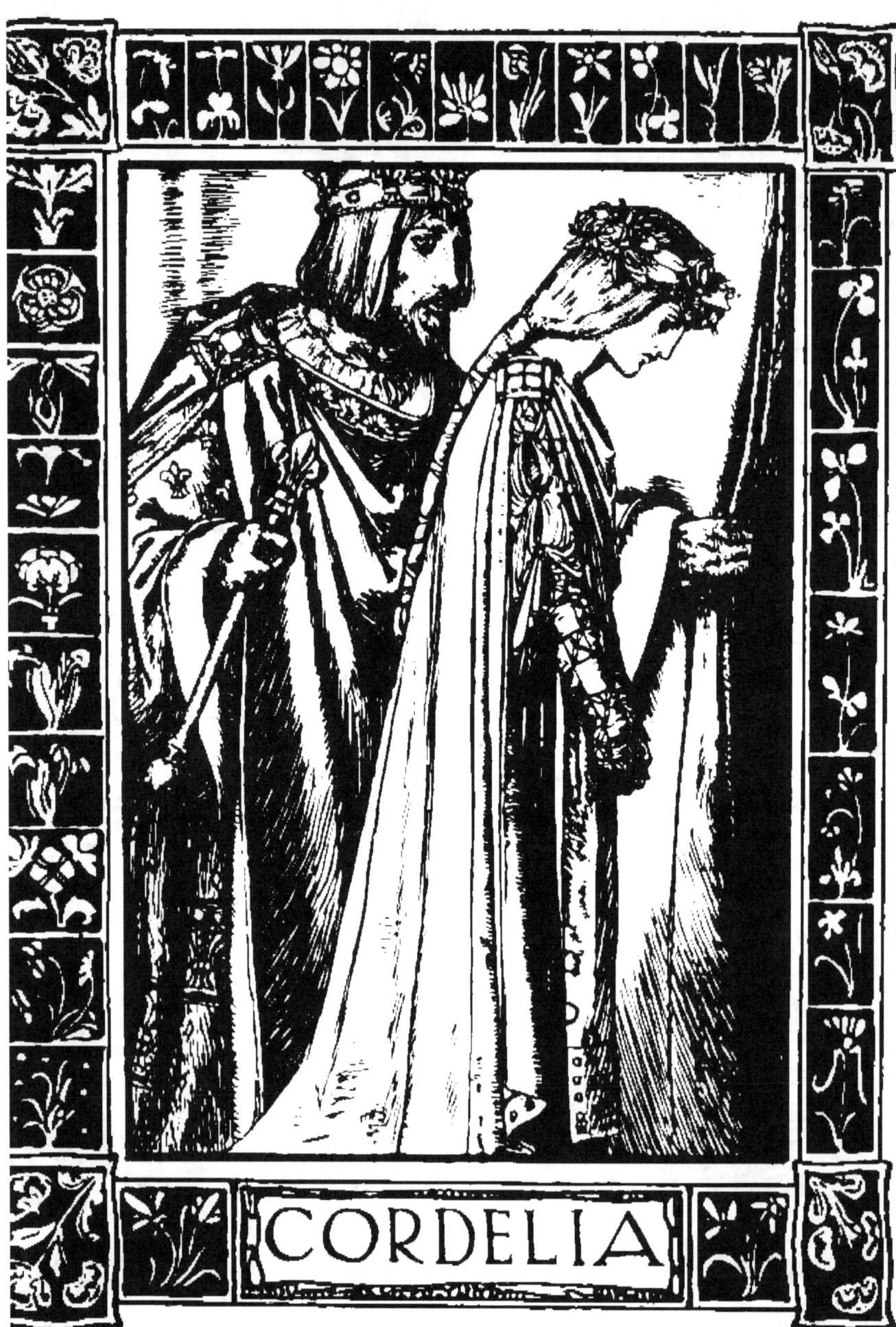

CORDELIA

CLEOPATRA

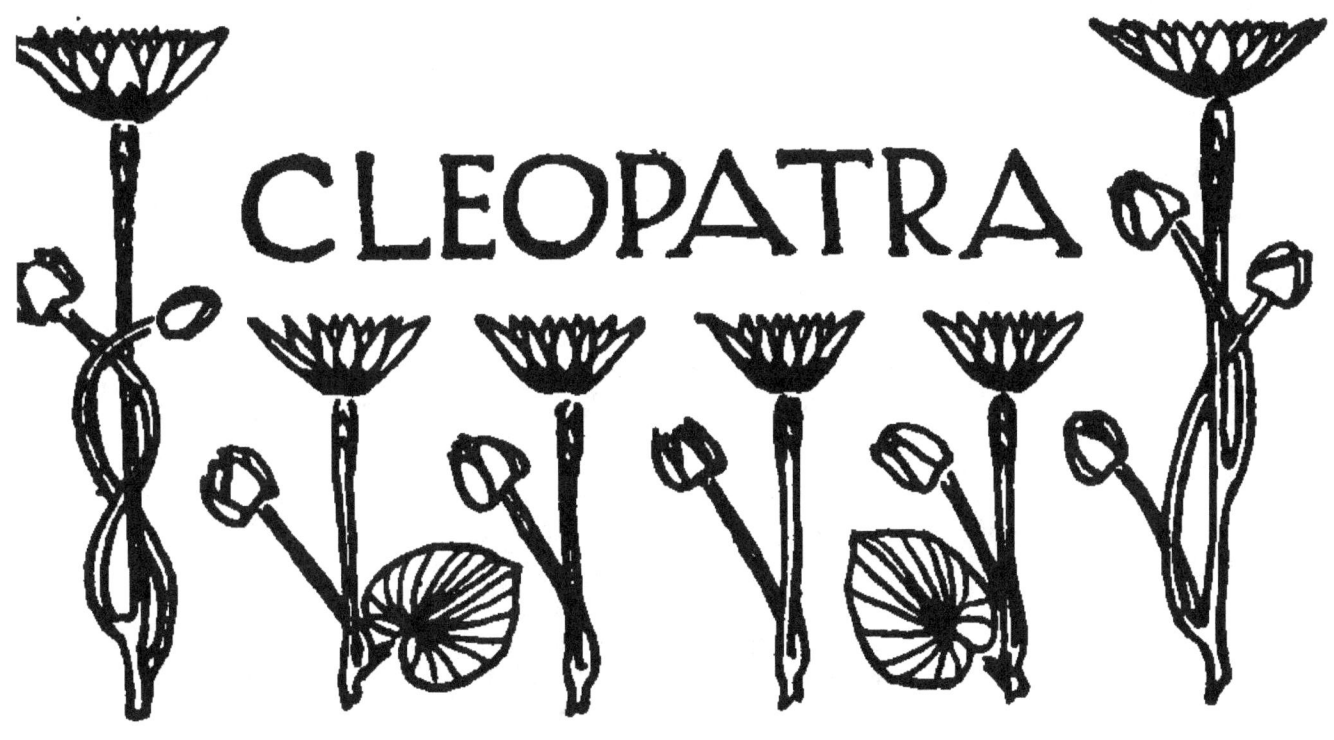

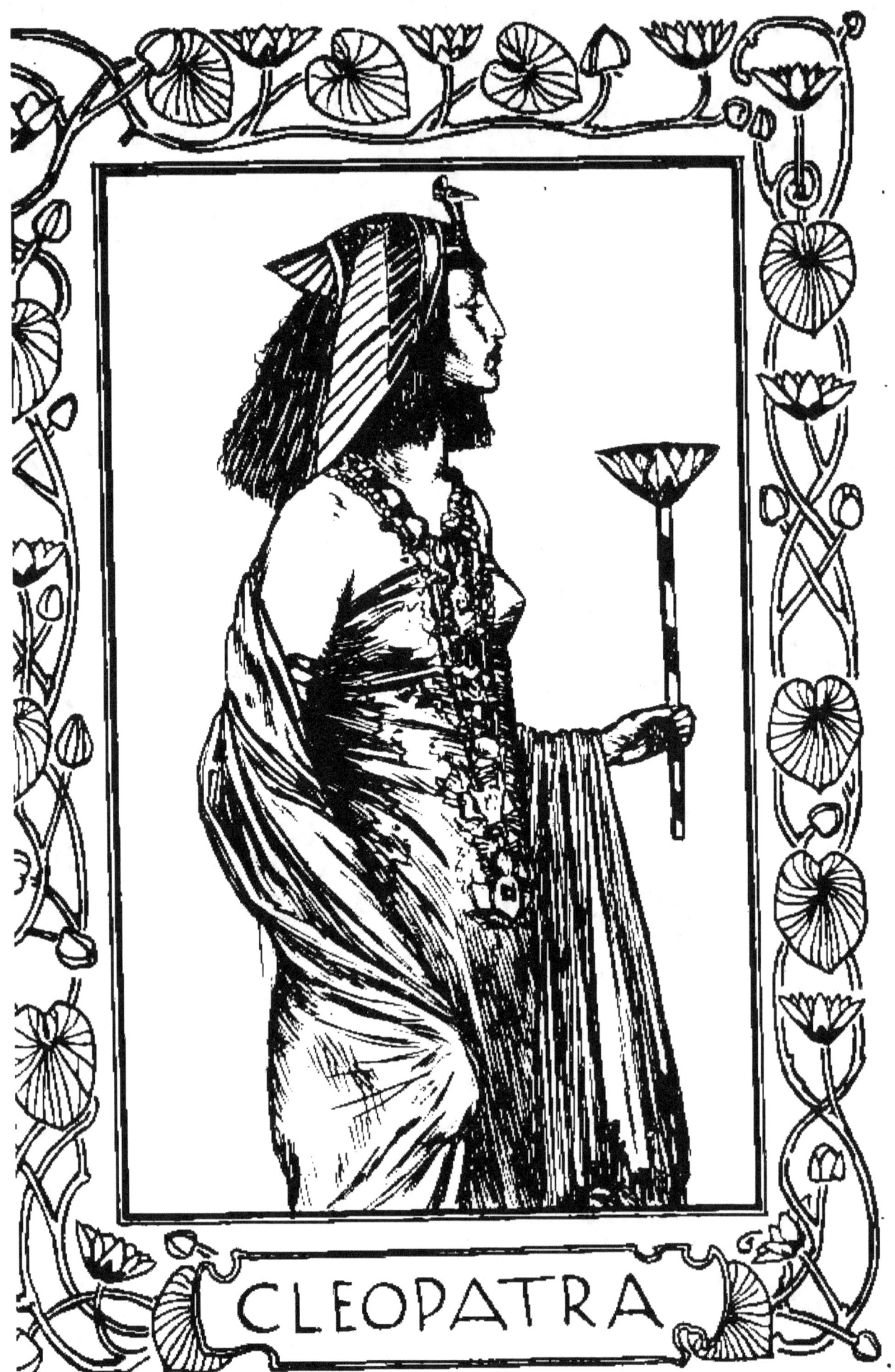

CLEOPATRA

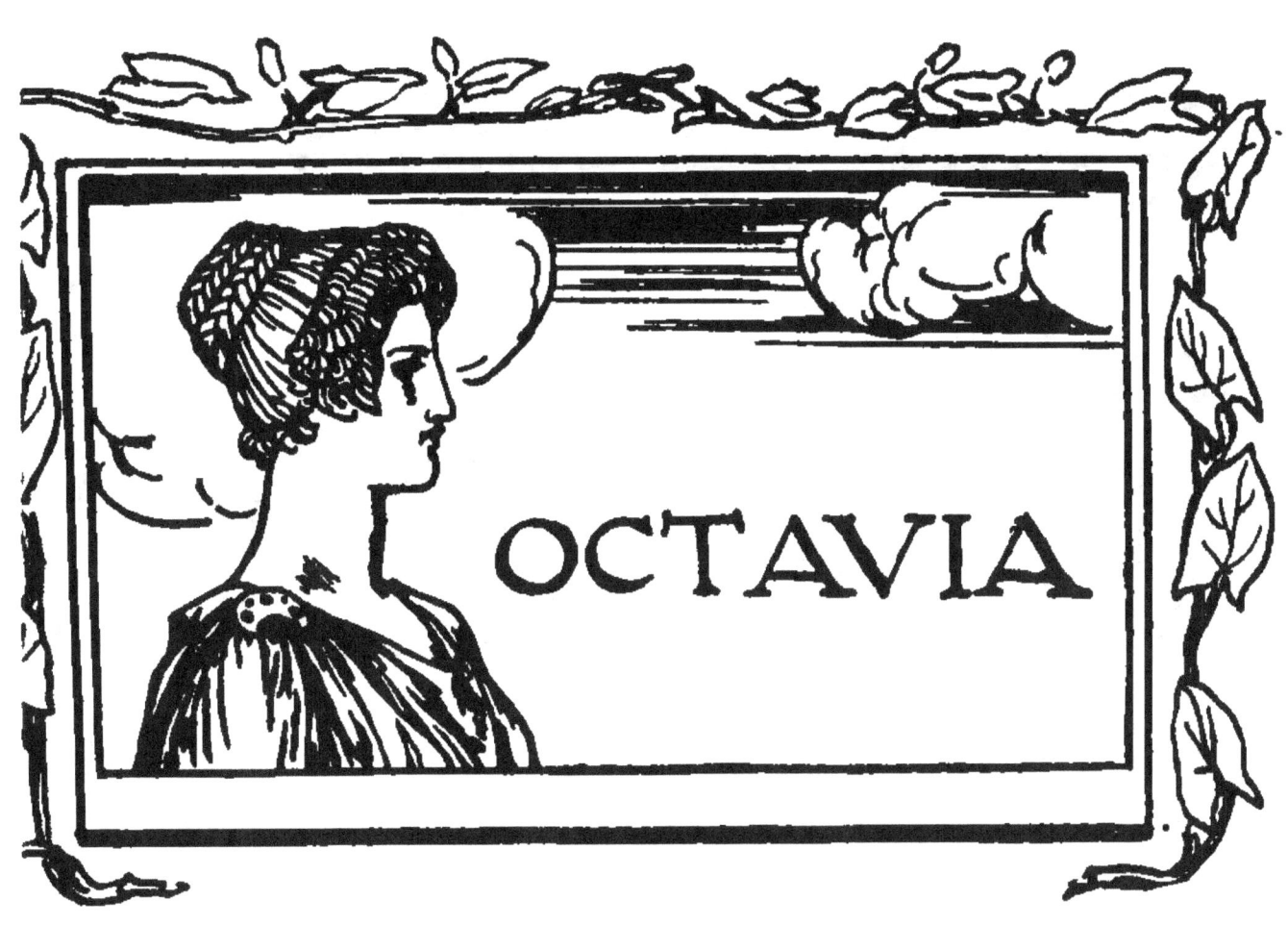

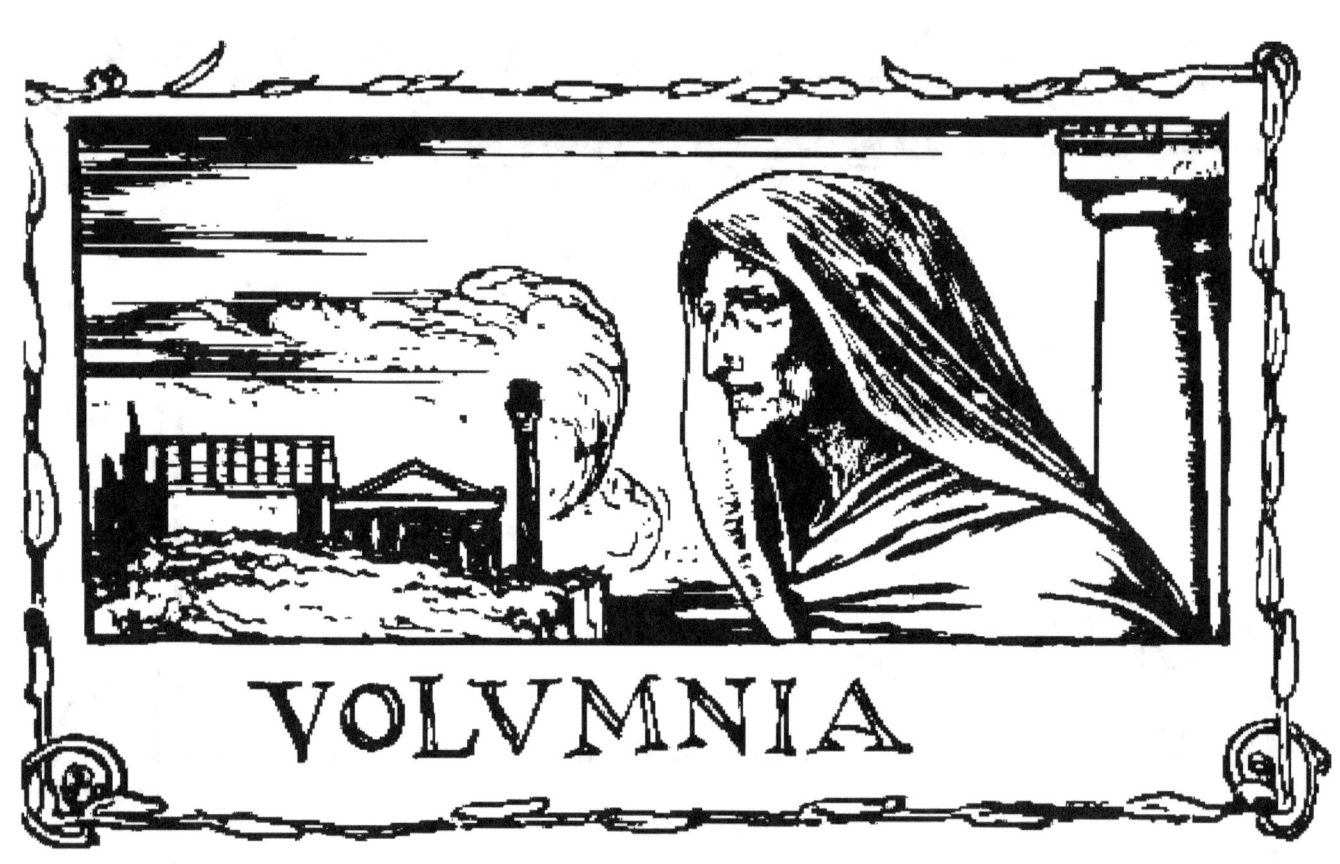

VOLVMNIA

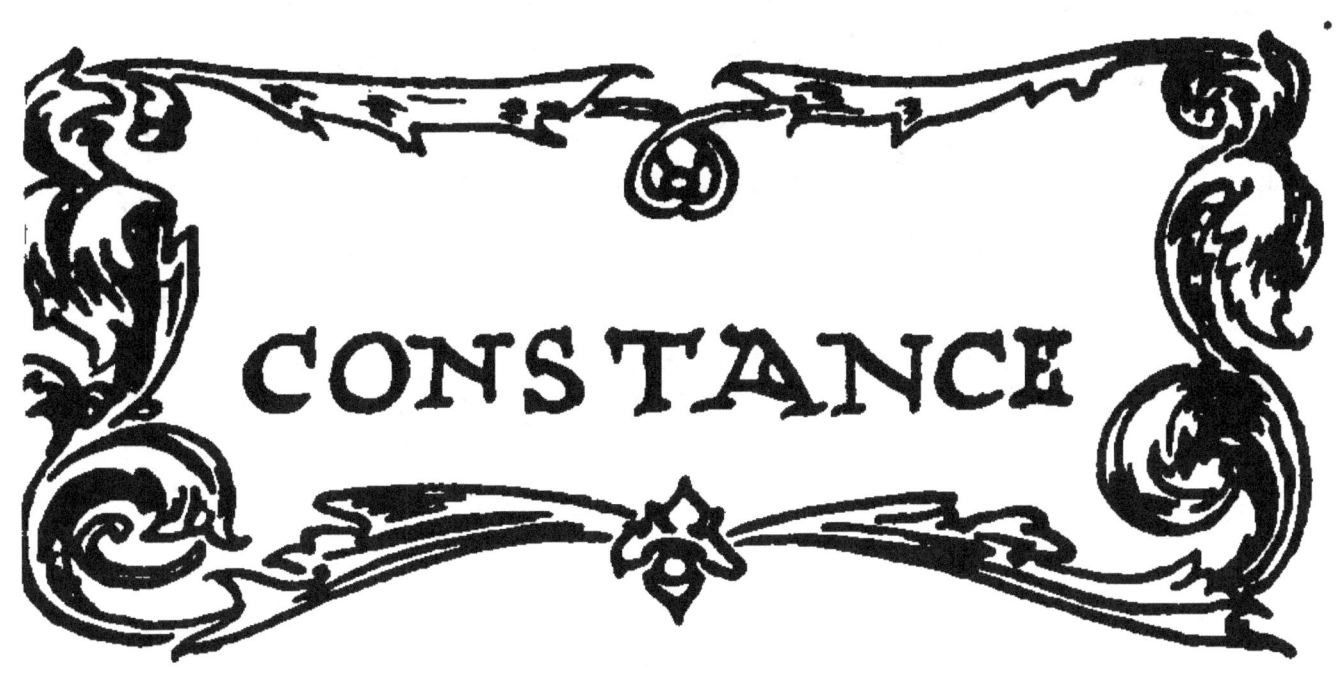

CONSTANCE

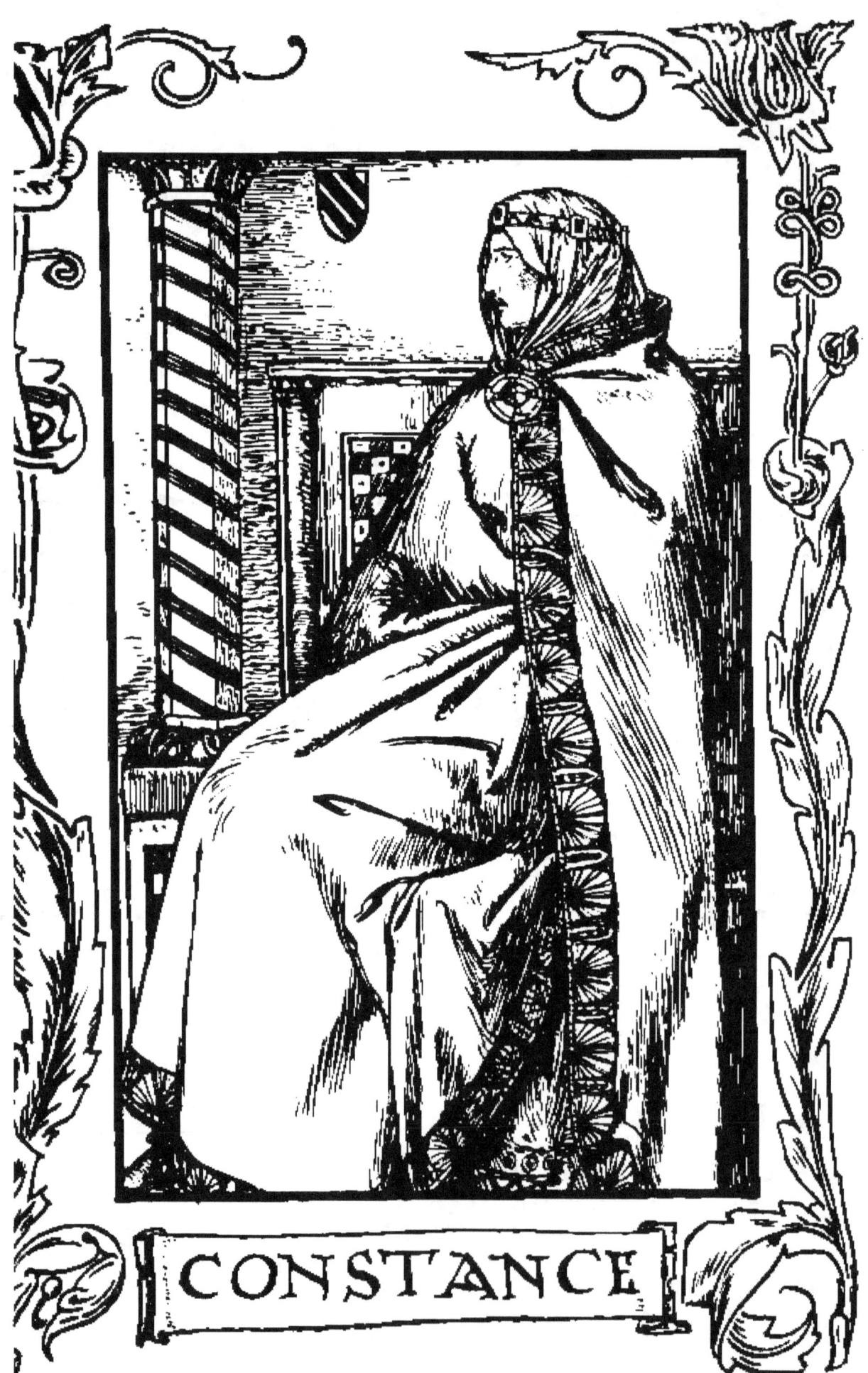

CONSTANCE

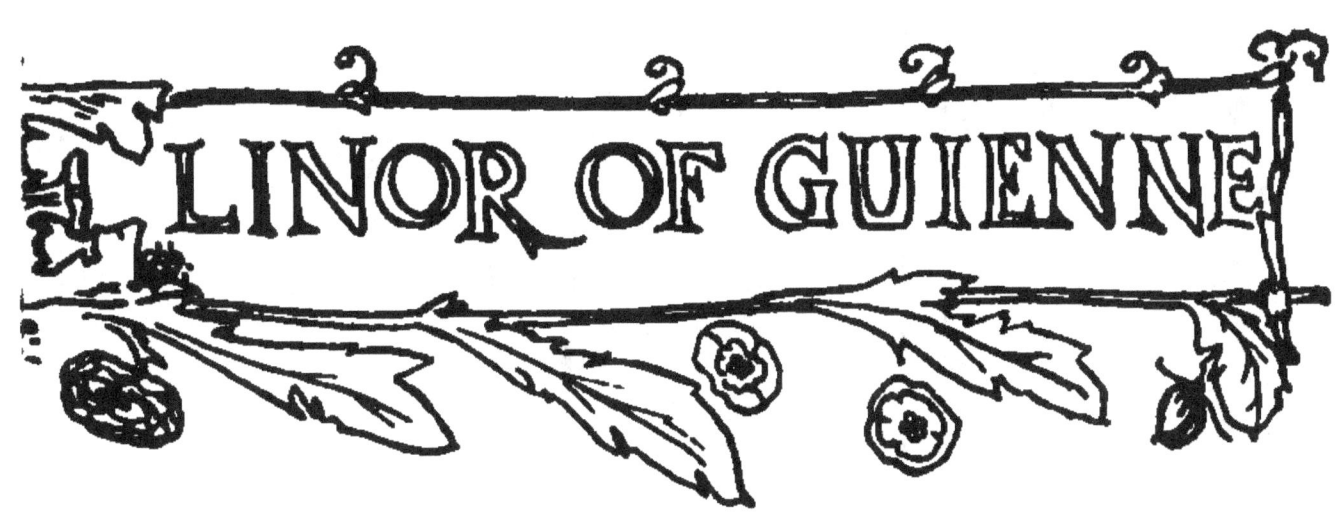

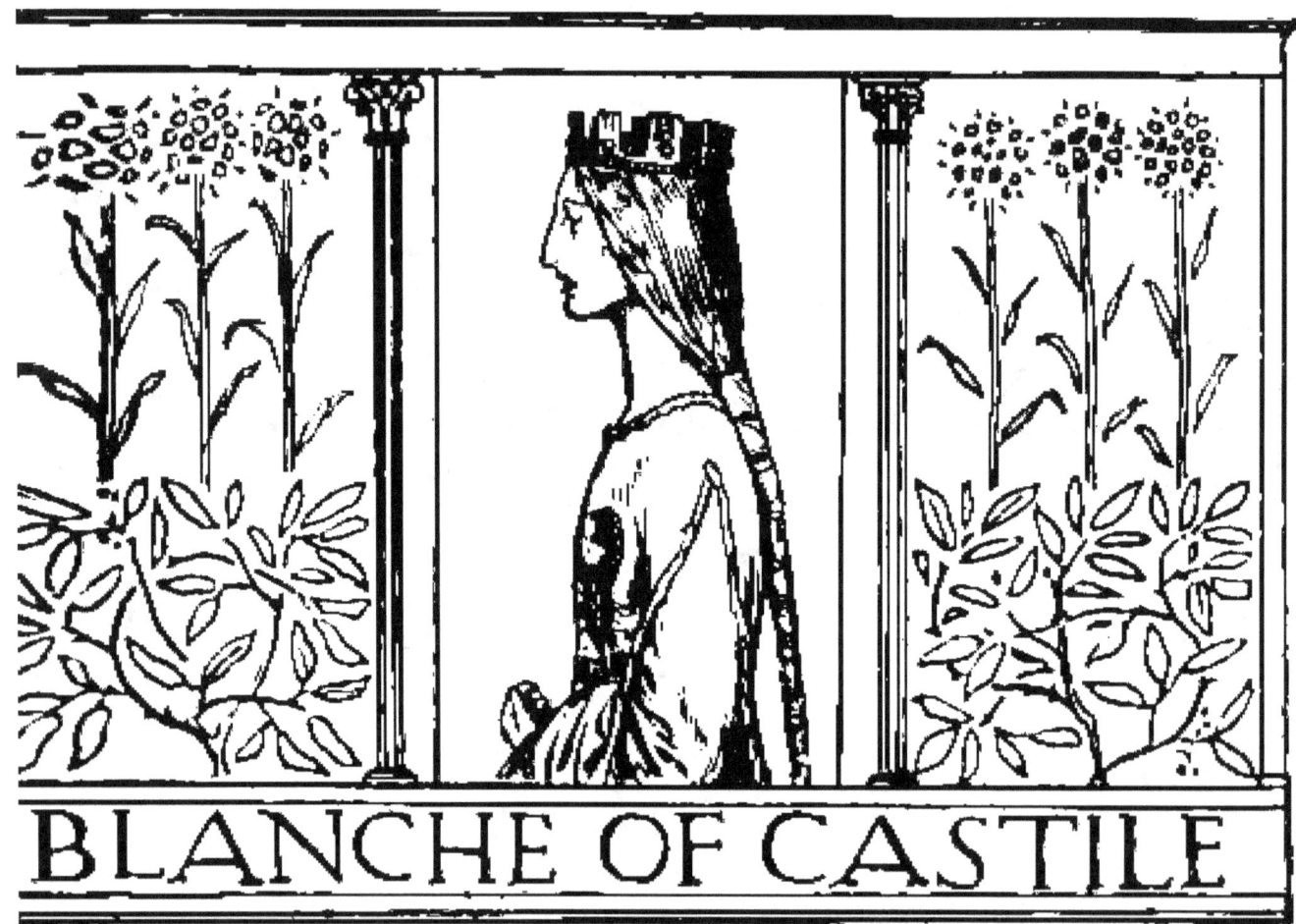

BLANCHE OF CASTILE

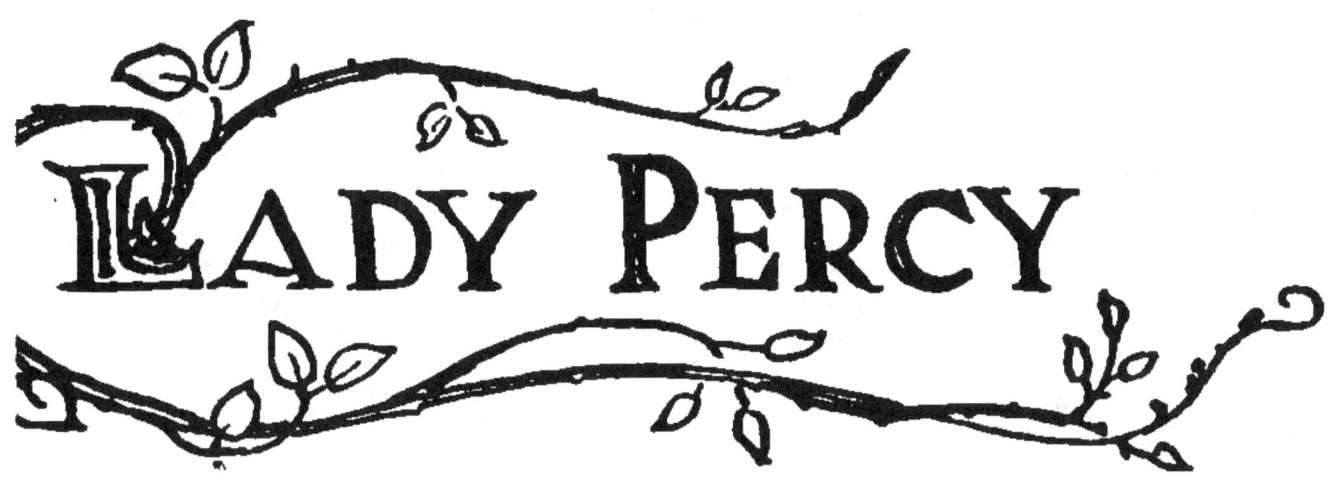

LADY PERCY

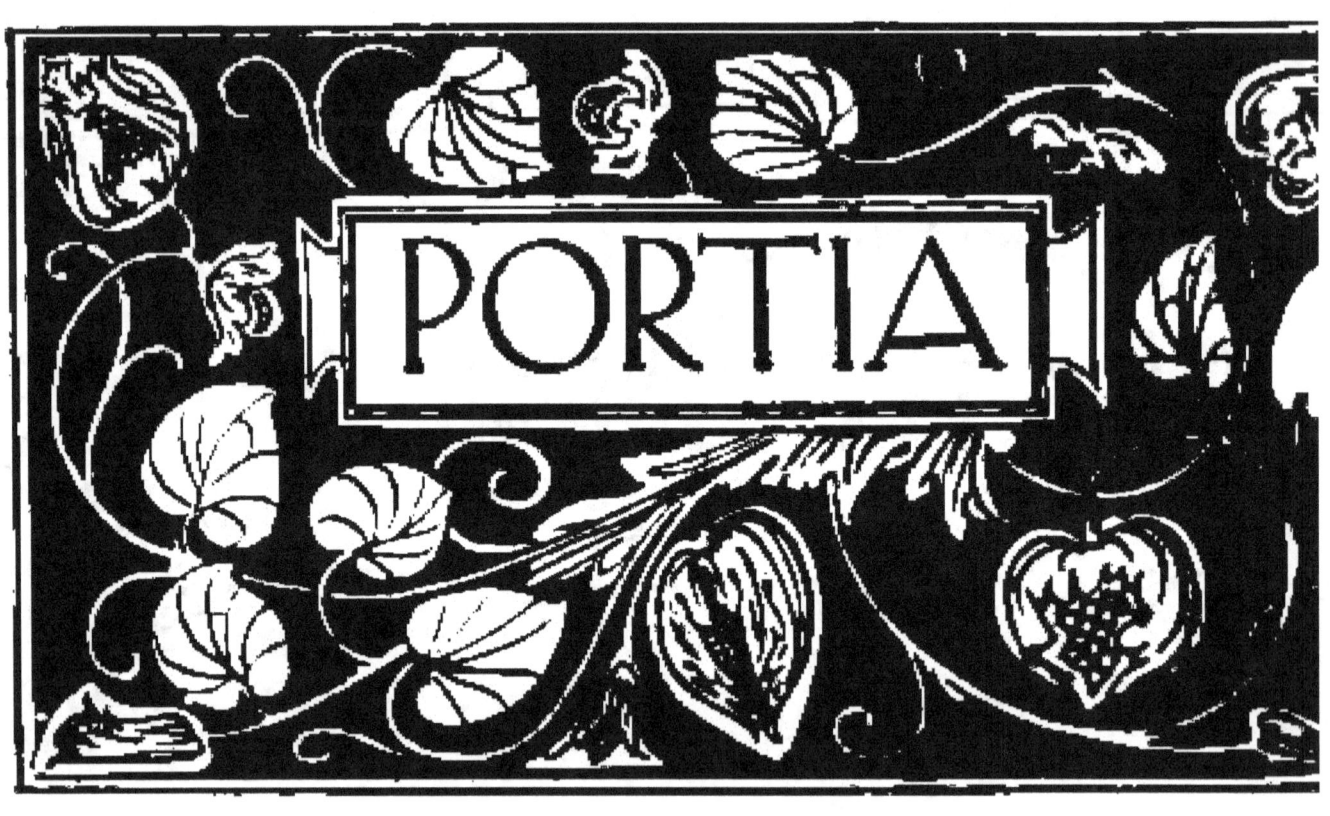

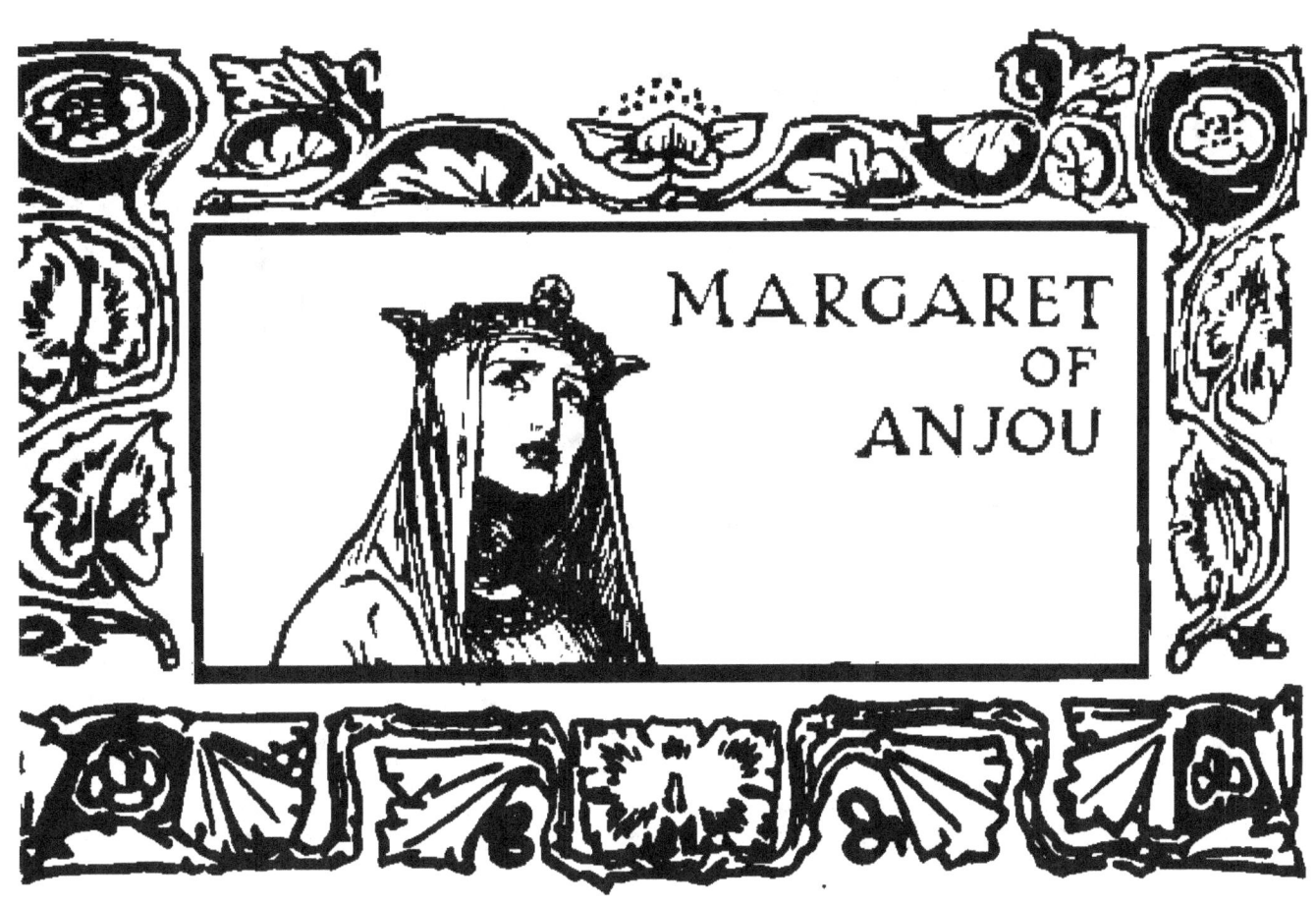

MARGARET
OF
ANJOU

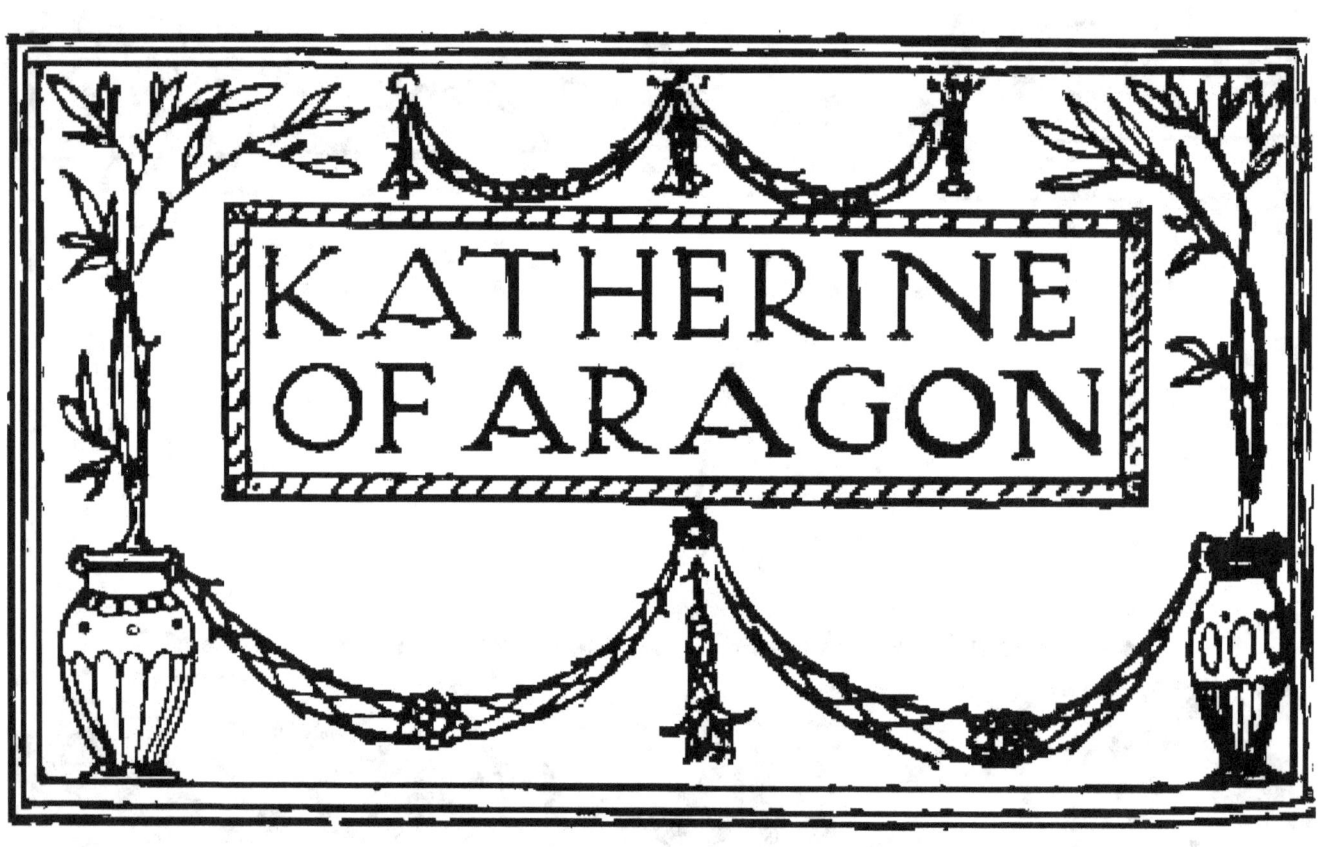

KATHERINE
OF ARAGON

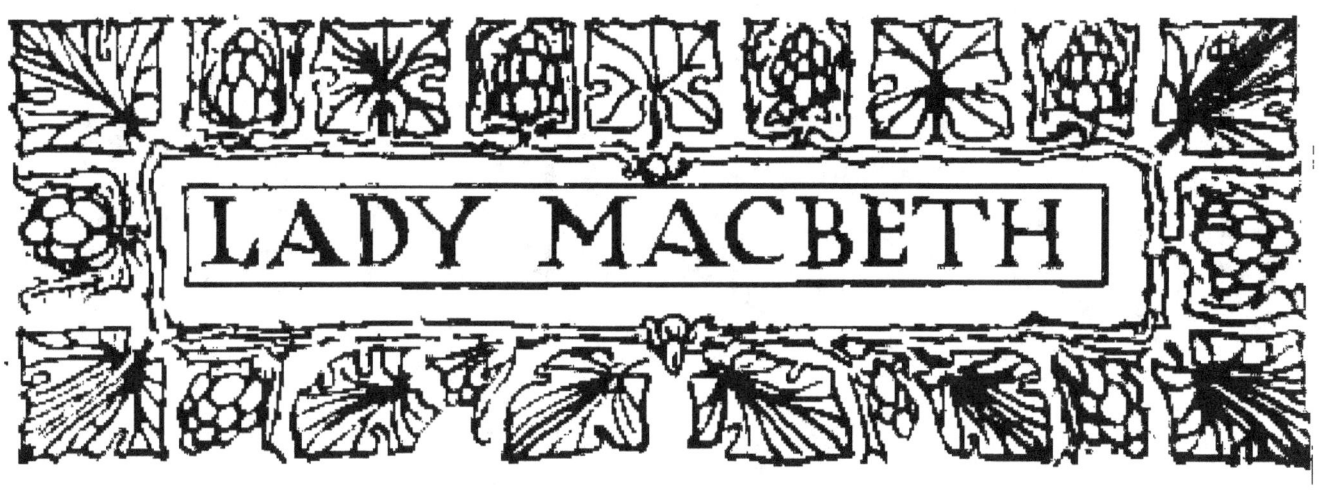

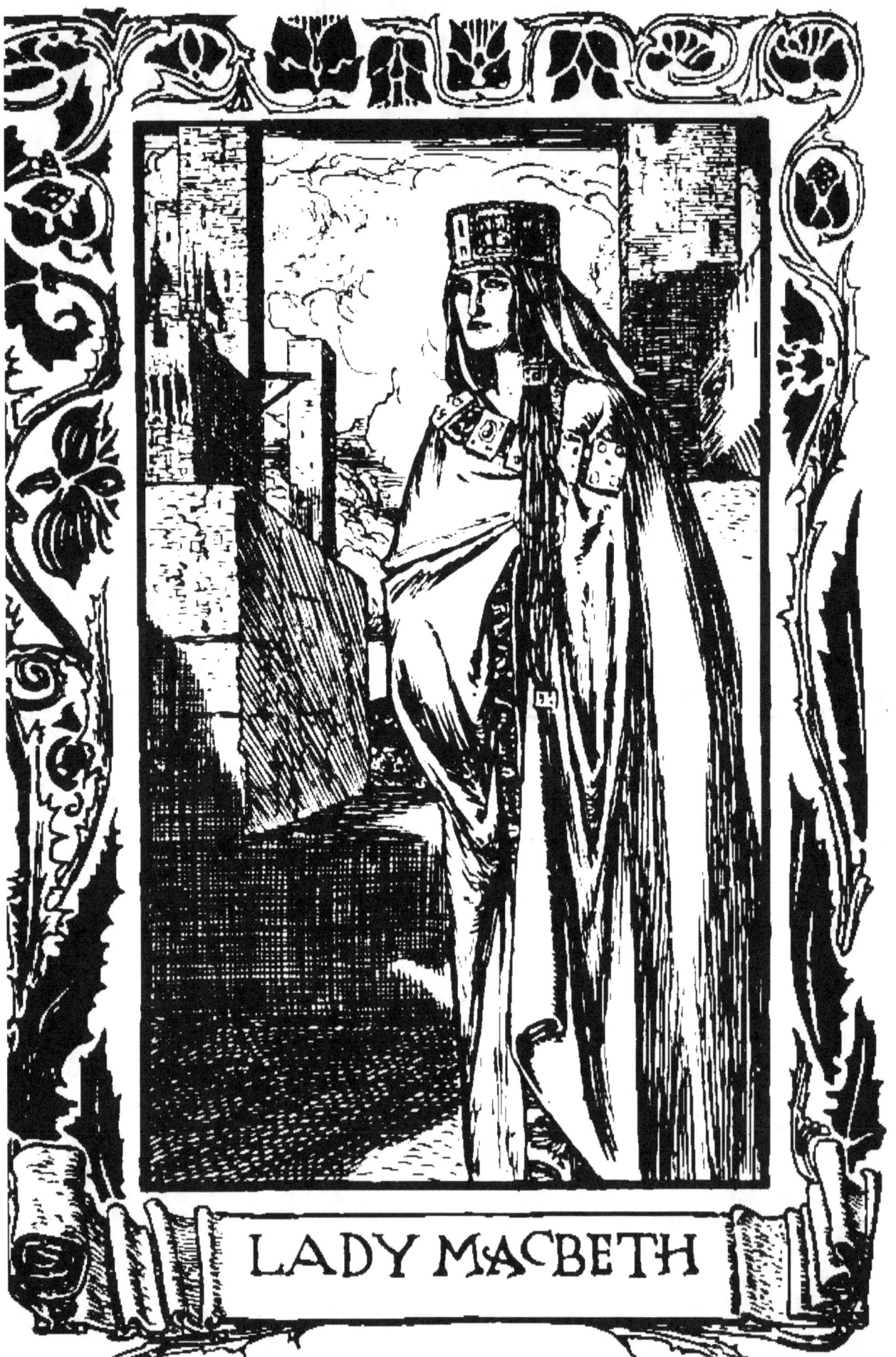

LADY MACBETH

www.ingramcontent.com/pod-product-compliance
Lightning Source LLC
Chambersburg PA
CBHW081622220526
45468CB00010B/2992